Religious violence has massive implications for Ch rooted in Christ's ethics of love, humility, compassi nonviolence. Mipo E. Dadang helps Christians in N not only the importance of paying attention to Christ's nonviolent teaching, but also how violent conflicts negatively shape and influence Christians in contexts of religious violence – to the extent that they can easily become unaware captives of a fanatical faith-based group. Dadang's work draws our attention to the fact that religious violence and current Christian responses are key issues facing Christianity in Nigeria and beyond. Dadang carefully and diligently addresses the implicit challenge posed by the continuous religious violence in Northern Nigeria, and he enables us to appreciate the gravity of the issues involved. He dissects and teases out the role of the Bible in helping Christians to correctly analyze, interpret, and explain the implications of any social-context bedeviled by religious violence. Towards a solution to the current dilemma and impasse, he specifically concentrates on describing and examining the trajectory of violent responses to religious violence among some Christians in Northern Nigeria. Dadang is deeply disturbed by the fact that instead of Nigerian Christians learning Christ's ethics of war – love, nonviolence, just-peacemaking, and so on – they are becoming influenced by their traditional world's method of responding to violent conflict. For Dadang, a way out of this impasse is to realize that, "Violence is a problem that the church needs to address if the church is to preach the gospel in a nonviolent environment" (p. 3). The plain truth is that some Nigerian Christians are yet to learn how to respond nonviolently. With the increasing ethnic, political, economic, and religious violent conflicts in Nigeria, the message of this book needs to be popularized and brought home to all Christian faiths and denominations.

Sunday Bobai Agang, PhD
Professor of Christian Ethics, Theology and Public Policy,
Provost, ECWA Theological Seminary, Jos

This book is one of a kind when it comes to addressing religious violence in Nigeria. It is a delightful guide full of important information for those of us who want to fully engage with handling the issue of religious violence. The book provides biblical and theological insights regarding the right response for believers in the context of religious violence. The book is not just theoretical but very engaging and practical in nature. The author provides deep theological conversations in an easy-to-read manner. The book provides the right theological response for believers in Northern Nigeria who are facing violent persecution on daily basis. The author grapples with both literature and personal experience to describe the reality of religious violence in Nigeria and gives theologically grounded ideas for practice that will build up the church in Northern Nigeria amidst violent persecution. I recommend this book to all theological institutions, families, youth workers, churches, and to all those who are concerned with religious violence around the globe.

Nathan H. Chiroma, PhD
Dean, School of Theology,
Pan Africa Christian University, Nairobi, Kenya

Mipo Dadang has experienced religious violence first hand, yet demonstrates in this penetrating study that such violence is not God's will, nor can it be justified biblically – no, not even in the portrayal of Yahweh in the Old Testament. In the death of Jesus all violence has been met and surpassed, providing the God-pleasing payment for the sins of the whole world. The book grapples with violence as a missiological problem and offers solutions that will benefit not only those directly affected in northern Nigeria, but all Christians everywhere.

John G. Nordling, PhD
Professor of Exegetical Theology,
Concordia Theological Seminary, Indiana, USA

Mipo Dadang has done a thorough job of addressing the issue of religious violence against believers in Jesus Christ in the Nigerian context. His thoughtful research drives home the point that God is sovereign over the affairs of men and that his children can respond supernaturally to suffering because of their trust in him. Dadang is very persuasive in his conclusions, using sound biblical theology to support them. He has personally experienced what he is writing about and that is what makes his arguments so forceful. I strongly encourage every believer to read this book, especially those who are currently going through persecution for their faith.

Marc Wooten, PhD
Adjunct Professor of World Religions,
Asia Biblical Theological Seminary, Philippines

A Cry For Help

A Missiological Reflection on Violent Response to Religious Tension in Northern Nigeria

Mipo E. Dadang

Published 2022 by Langham Monographs
An imprint of Langham Publishing
www.langhampublishing.org

Langham Publishing and its imprints are a ministry of Langham Partnership

Langham Partnership
PO Box 296, Carlisle, Cumbria, CA3 9WZ, UK
www.langham.org

ISBNs:
978-1-83973-572-1 Print
978-1-83973-686-5 ePub
978-1-83973-687-2 Mobi
978-1-83973-688-9 PDF

British Library Cataloguing-in-Publication Data
A catalogue record for this book is available from the British Library

ISBN: 978-1-83973-572-1

Cover & Book Design: projectluz.com

"Cast your cares on the Lord
and He will sustain you;
He will never let the righteous be shaken."
Psalm 55:22

Contents

Abbreviations

LW	Luther's Works
NLFA	New Life for All
TEKAN	Association of Christians in Nigeria
COCIN	Church of Christ in Nations
CAN	Christian Association of Nigeria
SIM	Sudan Interior Mission
CRK	Christian Religious Knowledge
O.I.C	Organization of Islamic Conference
ECWA	Evangelical Church Winning All
AEM	African Evangelism Mission
AIM	African Industrial Mission
FCS	Fellowship Christian Students
CMS	Church Missionary Society

Acknowledgments

I remain grateful to God for his unmerited grace and love of salvation upon me and for providing men and women with the various resources and professional skills I needed to complete the Doctor of Philosophy degree studies at Concordia Theological Seminary (CTS). Although the journey of my academic pursuit has been characterized by many challenges, God has been faithful. I want to thank God and people who surrounded me with consistent prayers and financial support. It has been your continuous and unshakable support that made it possible for me to translate my dream into reality.

This work would have not been completed without the help of my supervisor and adviser. I am most grateful to Dr. Klaus Detlev Schulz, dean of Graduate Studies and doctoral program in missiology supervisor, for your great wealth of experience and ability to provide sound holistic theological education and godly leadership as you direct the affairs of the doctoral program. Indeed, you are an exceptional teacher, mentor, and counselor. You have provided encouragement and inspirational motivation to me throughout, to the end of my doctoral studies at CTS.

My deepest appreciation goes to Cynthia Johnson, administrative assistant to the Graduate Studies and Chapel programs, for your godly treatment toward students in the PhD program. You are such a wonderful counselor, caring, compassionate, and full of God's love in your life. Thank you for the tender and holistic services you rendered to me. This provided an enabling learning environment that sustained me to the end of my study.

I am most grateful to my dissertation father, Dr. John Nordling, a diligent scholar in classics and a notable author, whose objective and constructive advice, guidance, and encouragement has made this research writing a scholarly one.

Professor David Coles, thank you for your global knowledge in historical theology and for impacting my student life at CTS in historical matters. I remain thankful to all the professors who taught me for their wealth of knowledge. I thank the registrar, Mrs. Barbara Wegman, for your careful guidance and for assisting me in registering for the courses I needed. I am thankful to Dr. Yohanness Mengsteap for inspiring me to develop the topic in your missiological research design class.

Barrister Pius A. Akubo, I thank you for becoming the first person to support my training. I sincerely appreciate all the pastors and elders of the following Evangelical Church Winning All (ECWA): Wuse II Garki Abuja, Maitama Abuja, Apapa Lagos. I am very grateful to Northridge Baptist Church, Cook Road, Fort Wayne, Immanuel World Outreach, Illinois, and ECWA USA, Chicago for your support toward my studies.

My deepest thanks go to my family for their understanding, support, patience, and endurance during the time I was absent from them for years to study. I thank my wife, Deborah Dadang, for your unending love, care, support, and spiritual virtue with which you have impacted my life throughout our years of fruitful marriage. If God were to allow marriage in eternity, I would marry you again. Thank you for believing in me and for encouraging me. I thank all my handsome sons and beautiful daughters that God has blessed us with. Alex and Lengnan, our sons, are deeply appreciated for always using every opportunity to pray for me and to assist me with errands. My appreciation equally goes to our daughters, Patience, Mercy, Nandi, and Keziah, for always giving your time to assist me in different ways when I had to travel for field research and for taking time to pray for my safety.

I want to further appreciate Mr. Alex and Nanep Ladan for the sacrificial financial support you gave me when I was stranded. I thank all individual Christian families that were willing to partner with me during the period of my study.

I deeply appreciate the former African Union Force Commander, General Martin Luther and Ruth Agwai (retired) for your financial support throughout the years of my studies. I am grateful to Honorable Justice Yargata Nimpar for your support and constant words of encouragement. There were times when I was discouraged, you shared from scripture to keep me going. To Honorable Justice Christine Dabup, I thank you for your support. It went a long way in helping me toward success. Mr. and Mrs. Clement Dalut, I thank you for your sacrificial financial support you gave.

I sincerely thank Dr. Istifanus and Mairo Zabadi for standing by me and especially for providing emergency support so that I could return to complete my school work. I thank you Mrs. Naomi Panya for asking your friends Mrs. Ruth Audu and Mrs. Kande Bala to support me financially and I thank you for asking Accelerated Christian Education to further support me. I thank Elder Joshua Maikori for your support. I thank Trustee Dr. Peter S. Abdu and Mrs. Helen Peter for your financial support.

I want to express deeply my profound gratitude to Rev. Silas and Binta Dauji for the tremendous financial help and other services you provided toward my studies. Binta, I thank you for the constant help you gave by driving me around places to buy food and other things I needed in and around Fort Wayne. You are a special gift and I thank you for all the services you rendered. I would like to appreciate architect Femi Offie for your support and encouragement.

I deeply appreciate your support toward my study Mr. and Mrs. John Gwani. Indeed, words cannot convey all you have done to see that I succeed. Prof. Bulus and Dr. Mrs. Rose Galadima, I do not know how to thank you, but God knows. I am grateful for the financial support you extended for my studies, despite the fact that you are in diaspora. I deeply thank Rev. Dr. Gideon Para-Mallam for taking it upon you to make contact so that I could make it to the end of my studies. I am most grateful to Da David Jonah Jang, the Governor of Plateau State. You not only gave me the opportunity to serve on one of your boards, but you also supported me toward my study.

Last, but not least, I want to thank the participants for their willingness to share their Christian experiences with me with such freedom and for their willingness to welcome me to their midst without notice. My special thank you goes to Mr. Aaron Frank, my companion, for his willingness to journey with me to the interview centers and for using his journalism skills in recording the information. I also thank you very much for using your car to transport both of us to carry out the field research work. I deeply appreciate all the district church leaders for demonstrating the spirit of African hospitality by their willingness to accommodate my interview schedule into their busy plans.

Abstract

The purpose of this research is to describe and examine the phenomenon of the violent responses to religious violence among some Christians in Northern Nigeria. The biblical narrative portion of the research examines the problem of violence beginning from the Old Testament on the basis of Genesis 4:8–10; 6:5–8; Psalm 10:15, 17–18; Isaiah 4:2; 9:6–7; Micah 4:3; and Joel 3:9–10. Examination of the Old Testament offers insight to the researcher. The major lesson pointed out from the facts examined is: the Hebrew Scripture is not a primer on violence. Rather, in surprising fullness and diversity, it provides guidance for overcoming violence and guides readers to hinder, reject, prevent, and eliminate its causes. The Old Testament portrays violence as abnormal, even pathological. Neither the original creation of Genesis 1–2 nor the eventual new creation of Revelation 21–22 has any place for violence; Old Testament literature gives hope of an ultimate end to violence so Yahweh is said to have worked violence that belongs to the enforcement of his sovereignty (Gen 3:15). Therefore, violence is not part of creation. Rather, violence is a result of the chaos, alienation, and pride of fallen humanity (Gen 3:1–14); and the prophets continued with the announcement of the future coming of the Prince of peace, who will establish the new kingdom of peace (Isa 4:2; 9:6; Mic 4:3, and Joel 3:9–10).

In New Testament literature, investigation reveals, according to Paul's teaching in his epistle to the Romans, that violence is replaced by creative, nonviolent alternatives (Rom 8:20–23). It is absorbed with patient suffering and forgiving love already realized in God's established kingdom through Jesus Christ (Luke 24:39; John 3:16, 4:24; and Heb 9:15). God's established kingdom through Jesus Christ never defined the mission of the New Testament church as the conquest of land and people. Violence results from and manifests human sin and rebellion against the Creator (Gen 3; Rom 3:23, 6:23). This position comes from the teaching of Jesus Christ in Matthew 5 and other passages from the Gospels (Luke 6:20–23, 27–31). Rather, Scriptures fulfilled Christ's death as foretold in the Old Testament. The sinless Son of God stands in the midst of these evils and allows violence to take place so he can redeem and free souls to the will of God to recognize all human beings as bearers of God's image in which all carnal weapons are renounced (Matt 26:50–56; 2 Cor 10:4–5). Jesus Christ has fully exhibited God's will in a violent world (John 19:30), calling Christians to peacemaking and patient suffering. Jesus Christ is the peace of Christians, who has made them one and ended hostility (Eph 2:14). A violent ending awaits Satan and his cohorts at the end of human history (Rev 19:11–15; 20:1–10).

Martin Luther's work has been extensively examined by the researcher and findings available show that Martin Luther did not condone the idea of violence no matter how just it might be. However, Luther cautions with regards to war among two equals saying that whoever starts a war is in the wrong. According to Luther, war is a matter of self-defense: "self-defense is the proper ground for fighting and therefore, all laws agree that self-defense shall go unpunished; he who kills another in self-defense is innocent in the eyes of all men."[1] In the essential literature, the researcher examined the early Christians' response to religious violence from the first through fourth centuries. The researcher also examined current scholarship that contributes in providing insight that helps in responding to the problem of religious violence in our society.

The field aspects of the study were ethnographic and phenomenological, except for the first research question, which is a historical study carried out among Christians in Northern Nigeria combined with participation observation. The researcher planned to have interviews with seven participants each from thirteen states using a semi-structured interview protocol. But seven participants died in religious violence before the interviews, leaving eighty-four participants interviewed. The participants were Christians. The researcher asked participants to describe the problem, causes, approaches, and response toward religious violence among the Christians in Northern Nigeria.

1. Luther's Works, Volume 46, *The Christian Society III*, 120, 121, 122, 123.

The researcher carried out pilot interviews in English and Hausa languages among the Christians in Northern Nigeria and Plateau state in Jos, central Nigeria. The purpose of the research was to examine why some Christians in Northern Nigeria have resorted to violent means in response to religious violence. The rationale to research the problem was a result of the bloody Muslim-Christian religious violence that for decades has continued unabated in Northern Nigeria. Four research questions were used to determine the understanding of why some Christians in Northern Nigeria have resorted to violent means in response to violence. These are (1) What was the social and religious context in which the Christians in Northern Nigeria were planted? (2) How do the Christians in Northern Nigeria describe what the Christian message means to them? (3) How do Christians in Northern Nigeria describe the cause (s) of religious violence? And (4) What solution to the problem of religious violence do Christians in Northern Nigeria propose?

The findings of this research affirm that resorting to violent means in response to religious violence is increasing among Christians in Northern Nigeria. The study confirms that there is one common reason for resorting to a traditional means of resisting violence – seeking powers from the spirits of their ancestors to safeguard their lives. They go outside of the church for assistance after not finding help in the church. The major headlines of the findings have the following components: (1) despair, desperation, and uncertainty; (2) pitfalls in worldviews; (3) problems of Pentecostal influence on young ECWA pastors in Nigeria; (4) problems of growth by numbers; (5) lack of love; (6) lack of forgiveness and reconciliation; and (7) adopting self-defense. The research shows that pastors, leaders, missionaries, and parachurch organizations should acknowledge the need to have a biblical basis and theological perspective involved in the entire phenomenon of resorting to violent means and should be more conscious and purposeful in addressing issues of violence in their teaching, applying the right homiletical principles in pulpit ministries. The church "must learn to listen in order to respond to cries and the crises of our time." But if government forces fail to protect the lives and property of citizens by its irresponsibility, Christians should not fail to defend themselves, family members, and property, if they are attacked violently, as in war.

CHAPTER ONE

Violence as a Missiological Problem

This missiological research problem concerns violence and ecclesiology, which traces a traditional biblical and historical literature review, analysis and evaluation, and then a long field research section, beginning with a methodological understanding of the field research. This is then followed by a joint conclusion of the literature and field research.

"The church is the focal point of Christian faith; the study of whose doctrine is referred to as ecclesiology."[1] In Greek, this designates a local congregation; the English word "church" is derived from the Greek *kyriakos* meaning the Lord's house.[2] In today's meaning, it is used sometimes collectively to refer to the New Testament church or the early saints. To this end, the church could be rightly seen as the body of the Lord Jesus Christ.[3] Hence, the Lord Jesus Christ, before his departure, gave one of the most important commands to his disciples: that they should go into the entire world and preach the gospel to all nations baptizing them in the name of the Father, Son, and Holy Spirit and teaching them to obey everything he had commanded (Matt 28:19–20).

Since the research problem concerns ecclesiology, it also falls within the classical theological disciplines that require attention in a religiously violent environment.[4] Tremendous church growth emerged in Africa. Douglas Jacobsen writes that Christianity was born in the Middle East and Jerusalem was the headquarters of the movement, but the new faith quickly spread

1. Gutip, *Church of Christ in Nigeria*, 51.
2. Gutip, 51.
3. Gutip, 51.
4. Schulz, *Mission from the Cross*, 33.

beyond Palestine.[5] From there, Christianity spread into Africa and Asia: "It was in Africa before Europe, it was in India before England, and it was in China before America."[6] Thus, "The headline story of Christianity in Africa can be summed up in one word: growth. Never before has Christianity expanded so quickly in any region of the world and today, there are more than 400 million Christians in the African Region."[7] Three major religious traditions flourish in Africa: Islam, Christianity, and African Traditional Religion. And yet Christianity has strong claims to be reckoned the oldest of the three traditions, with a continuous history on the continent of nearly 2,000 years.[8]

Andrew Walls notes that "at the end of the twentieth century, Africa was appearing as the Christian heartland."[9] He says,

> Growth is not just a transplant from the west, but the development of an authentic African religion which coincided with the retreat of Christianity in the West; has now moved to being a major component of contemporary, representative Christianity; the standard Christianity of the present age, a demonstration model of its character.[10]

However, the fact that Christianity in Africa so decisively collapsed in the face of Islam poses difficult historical and theological problems for Christianity in general and African Christianity in particular.[11] Jacobsen stresses that sub-Saharan Africa has been characterized by hope, despair, and social ills leading to violence.[12]

Michael Grant points out that "violence can hardly be gainsaid."[13] Leon Hardy Canfield writes, "There has been nothing approaching a consensus either among the faith traditions collectively or within each one individually as to how violence should be viewed from a religious perspective."[14] He

5. Jacobsen, *World's Christians*, 67.
6. Gilbert and Marshall, *Their Blood Cries Out*, 7.
7. Jacobsen, *World's Christians*, 163.
8. Hastings, *World History of Christianity*, 192.
9. Walls, *Cross-Cultural Process*, 118.
10. Walls, 119.
11. Hastings, *World History of Christianity*, 194.
12. Jacobsen, *World's Christians*, 155–57.
13. Grant, *World of Rome*, 1.
14. Canfield, *Early Persecution of the Christians*, 17.

further suggests "religion has always been the special center of intolerance and violence because its content is more highly valued by society than that of other departments of social life such as politics or philosophy."[15] Conflict in the later part of twentieth century has often been focused on the Sahelian belt of countries like Sudan and Nigeria.[16] Similarly, Robert Conquest tagged the twentieth century "the ravaged century" and "one of the bloodiest in human history in which Christians were major victims of war and violence."[17] Anyone who has ever experienced violence knows that it is not pleasant and would prefer that there be no mention of violence in any given society.[18] Hastings contends that "violence has always been present in society and may always be so until humankind shares identical intellectual convictions."[19] For a society, violence will always breed insecurity, never arriving at truth, justice, or equilibrium, but always reproducing endless counter violence.[20] In Africa, there have been ethnic and religious conflicts in Rwanda, Somalia, Ethiopia, Eritrea, Angola, Sudan, Liberia, Ivory Coast, the Democratic Republic of Congo, and Nigeria. Thompson summarizes the African situation as follows: "The continent of Africa is filled with conflicts, wars from south to north, west to east, fighting burns or simmers in Africa."[21]

Violence is a problem that the church needs to address if the church is to preach the gospel in a nonviolent environment. Indeed, the church in Africa has to create an understanding concerning the nature of this violence in order to respond well to its challenges. Violence has been a serious threat to the church and at the same time a global missiological problem, which Christians in Northern Nigeria and the world have faced throughout history. In the beginning, when God created man and placed him in the garden of

15. Canfield, 17.

16. Hastings, *World History of Christianity*, 231. "The Sahelian kingdoms were a series of kingdoms or empires that were centered on the sahel, the area of grasslands south of the Sahara. The wealth of the states came from controlling the trade routes across the desert." Wikipedia, s.v. "Sahelian Kingdoms," last modified 24 April 2021, http://en.wikipedia.org/wiki/Sahelian_kingdoms.

17. Conquest, *Reflections on a Ravaged Century*, 300–305.

18. Adrian Hastings laments the effect violence can have on a society. Hastings, *World History of Christianity*, 137.

19. Hastings, 1247.

20. Hastings, 1247.

21. Thompson, *Justice and Peace*, 136.

Eden (Gen 1:26, 27), humankind was living in the abundant "shalom," full of "completeness, soundness and wholeness."[22] But man's sin corrupted God's plan from that perfect and peaceful existence (Gen 3:8–14) and the perfect peace was destroyed. However, Yahweh promised hope of a future peace wherein humankind will experience restoration of peace (Gen 3:15). God told Adam and Eve to depart from the peaceful garden into a life full of chaos (Gen 3:23). Therefore, the life that God created for peaceful living was soon battered by violence (Gen 4:8). From then onward, histories of mankind became characterized by conflicts and violence. This violence continued to progress in human life until God ended the world in which Noah and the people of his own society lived (Gen 6:11).

In Leviticus, Kleinig notes that "the material in 19:17–18 presupposes a tribal society made up of close blood clans, a society governed by payback. In such a society each offense had to be avenged to preserve the society's social and moral ecology."[23] Payback operated positively as benefaction within the blood clan. It also operated negatively as revenge and hatred against those who stood outside it. The Lord therefore undermined the cycle of revenge by forbidding hatred and commanding love for all members of the Israelite congregation.[24] God forbade any person who had been injured to hate the offender secretly in his heart. Instead, he was required to confront the offender openly and directly with his offense. He was to rebuke his fellow Israelite to give him a chance to admit his wrongful deed and put it right.[25] If, however, anybody failed to reprimand the wrongdoer, but hated him instead and plotted his downfall, that person became a party to that evil deed. Hatred of the wrongdoer turned the victim into a wrongdoer. It devoured the hateful person.[26] The offended person was therefore required to rebuke the wrongdoer or else he himself would be guilty of hatred and suffer the penalty of hatred.[27] Kleinig concludes, "We are not told what the penalty was. It is, however, clear that such a person came under God's judgment."[28]

22. Feinberg, "Peace," 896.
23. Kleinig, *Leviticus*, 412.
24. Kleinig, 412.
25. Kleinig, 412.
26. Kleinig, 412.
27. Kleinig, 412.
28. Kleinig, 412.

The prohibition of vengeance in 19:18 follows directly from the prohibition of hatred in 19:17, for the desire for revenge and the nursing of grudges were the products of hatred. Even if the reproof of the evildoer did not produce a positive response, the Lord did not permit his people to take revenge, or even bear a grudge against the evildoer.[29] God alone paid back evildoers (Ps 94:1; Nah 1:2) and bore a grudge against them (Ps 103:9; Jer 3:5, 12; Nah 1:2). These two prohibitions contradicted the most basic tenet of a tribal society, the principle of personal retaliation. Those who had been injured could neither pay back the offender by an extra-judicial act of retribution, nor could they even indulge in secret mental scenarios of hatred and revenge.[30] All thoughts of revenge and acts of vengeance were equally forbidden. Instead, they were required to practice positive retaliation by showing love to those who had wronged them. The Israelites were required to treat those who wronged them as well as they treated themselves.[31] The love that the Lord commands is not basically an emotional attitude, a matter of sentiment, but an act of benevolence, a matter of the will, for feelings cannot be commanded. The Lord commands his people to act in a loving way toward their neighbors and care for them as they care for themselves.[32] This commandment does not, then, promote self-love, as if people had to love themselves before they could love others. Instead, it assumes that all people seek their own advantage, their own good, and do so without limitation or discrimination. Thus, Kleinig maintains that

> The neighbor who was to be loved in this way was most obviously an Israelite wrongdoer. But, as shown in 19:34, it also extended to the aliens resident with the Israelites in the land. Benevolent love was therefore to replace malevolent hatred as the response to slights and acts of injustice.[33]

All the prohibitions in this section culminate in the commandment to love the neighbor as oneself. This is the basic social duty of the Israelites as God's

29. Milgrom, *Leviticus 17–22*.

30. Kleinig, *Leviticus*, 412.

31. Kleinig, 412.

32. Kleinig, 412.

33. Kleinig, 413.

holy people, for God's holiness encouraged and fostered brotherly love in his congregation.[34]

The kind of loving benevolence that applied to close blood relatives in a tribal society was extended to the whole congregation of Israel. All its members were to be regarded as close spiritual kinsfolk, holy brothers and sisters in Lord's holy family, people who all shared equally in God's holiness and who all equally came under its protection. In the Psalms, the subject of violence is directed with questions and laments. The Psalmist raises a theological question, "Why, LORD, do you stand far off? Why do you hide yourself in times of trouble?" (Ps 10:1). Although the Psalmist recognizes God's presence, the knowledge connected to the events leading to his trouble is met with great difficulty; theological understanding appears so baffling and so hard to grasp. The Psalmist confidently prays that God will root out those who are wicked and take advantage of the weak and poor throughout Israel so that the wicked may not strike violence anymore (10:18). Such behavior, David reminds us, will be called to account. There is hope, however, whether we have taken advantage of the weak or have been victim of oppression. The Lord has compassion on those oppressed by sin. The Psalmist cries to God to "break the arm of the wicked" and evildoers and eradicate violence that resonates in the world (10:15). Chilton points out that this "is part of biblical heritage at the heart of Judaism, Christianity, and Islam."[35]

The teaching of nonviolence moves to the New Testament where the people of God are aliens, pilgrims, and ambassadors among the nations of the world (2 Cor 5:18). In place of a spirit of grudging recompense and quick revenge, Jesus calls his disciples to lives of joyful generosity and real forgiveness. His teaching was hyperbolic but does not mean that he is not unserious. Jesus embodied his teaching with such willing nonresistance and self-sacrifice presenting that his kingdom is not of this world (John 18:36), not murder (Matt 5:21–23), calling is his disciples to be faithful in the face of violence (Matt 10:28), and to respond as peacemakers to violence (Matt 5:9). This is will subsequently be discussed in chapter 2.

34. Kleinig, 413.

35. Chilton, *Abraham's Curse*, 46.

Historical Background of Nigeria

Nigeria is one of the West African countries situated by the coastal shore. Politically, the country has thirty-six states with its capital in Abuja. For political reasons, Nigeria is grouped into six geopolitical zones – South South, South East, South West, North Central, North East, and North West. Nigeria is a country with the world's largest African population, located on the Atlantic coast of West Africa, sharing borders with Benin, Niger, Chad, and Cameroon.[36] There are over 3,500 ethnic groups in Africa speaking different languages and practicing different cultures.[37] In Nigeria, the Operation World database and publication states, there are over 490 ethnic groups and it is one of the largest countries in Africa, by area, covering 356,669 square miles.[38] Nigeria is the most populous, the most recent census gives the official total population as 140,003,542, out of which 67,481,707 (48.2 percent) are Christians.[39] Nigeria, as a British Colony up until 1960, speaks English as its official language, along with other major languages. The major language groups spoken are Hausa, Fulani, Ibo, Yoruba, Kanuri, Ibibio, Effik, Tiv, Itsekiri, Ijaw, Edo, Annang, Nupe, Urhobo, Igala, Edoma, Gwagi, Berom, Jabba, Ngas, Taroh, Miship, Afezere, and Ankwai.[40]

Levin categorically states that Nigeria's artificial and consequent focus on promoting national identity brought alliance between Lord Lugard's concept of "indirect rule" and the Sokoto Caliphate's desire for a united states through culture and religion, "a vision of conquest and conversion, and after the amalgamation of the Northern, Western, and Eastern regions to become one Nigeria."[41] The *Operation World* database publication provides some statistics. Johnstone and Mandryk note that "three main regions, the Eastern, Northern and Western emerged as a result of colonial policy."[42] The British retained the pre-colonial Hausa-Fulani Muslim feudal rulers of the north

36. Gates and Appiah, *Africana*, 1432.

37. Johnstone and Mandryk, *Operation World*, 20.

38. Johnstone and Mandryk, 20.

39. This detail is in the official census report, which was carried out in 2006.

40. Otite and Ogionwo, *Introduction to Sociological Studies*, 152.

41. Levin, "New Nigeria," 134–44.

42. Johnstone and Mandryk, *Operation World*, 493. See also Oyewole, *Historical Dictionary of Nigeria*, 3.

and allowed them to extend their rule over the peoples of the Middle Belt, few of whom were Muslims at that time.[43]

Religious Worldviews

Johnstone and Mandryk provide a breakdown of religious identities in Central, North East and North West of Northern Nigeria. The Central Zone has an area of 266,617 square kilometers, a population 20,800,000, and 230 languages, with most using Hausa as their trade language. Christianity is 55 percent, Islam 30 percent, and Traditional Religion 15 percent.[44] The Northeast core has an area of 272,395 square kilometers and a population of 15,000,000. Islam is 50 percent, Traditional Religion 30 percent, and Christianity 20 percent.[45] The Northwest has an area of 191,873 square kilometers, and a population 23,800,000. Islam is 67 percent, Traditional Religion 20 percent, and Christianity 13 percent. Together, the Central Belt, the Northeast, and the Northwest form Northern Nigeria.[46]

African Worldview

The religious ideas and concepts in African Traditional Religion differ from one local community to another. Gehman notes, "It would be helpful if every group in Africa would know and understand their traditional beliefs."[47] These religious beliefs and practices include: belief in a supreme being, concept of man, and the worship of divinities, spirits, and ancestors. This understanding is not different from the Nigerian religious context. Adekoya admits "There is no doubt that there is a revival of African Traditional Religion. The low percentage of followers of traditional religion usually portrayed today is not a true reflection of reality."[48] According to Adekoya, Muslims and Christians reverted to traditional religion during the Jos, Plateau State religious violence.[49] African traditional religion has been described in different terms as animism,

43. Johnstone and Mandryk, *Operation World*, 493.
44. Johnstone and Mandryk, 493.
45. Johnstone and Mandryk, 493.
46. Johnstone and Mandryk, 494.
47. Gehman, *African Traditional Religion*, 3.
48. Adekoya, "The Religious Background", 8.
49. Adekoya, 8.

witchcraft, idolatry, paganism, heathenism, juju, fetishism, and primitive religion. Adekoya believes that

> traditional religion is the most comprehensive title for the religion of Africa because it gives the fullest meaning. The first is that the religion is distinctly African. The second is that it is really traditional, as it is the handing down of information, beliefs and customs by word of mouth or by example from one generation to another without instruction.[50]

Parrinder observes that traditional religion should not be spoken of in plural, although there are numerous types of religious practices among different people groups "because the similarities are far greater and more important than the differences."[51] Idowu notes that "man really finds little satisfaction except in a deity who lives, who has a heart, who speaks, who hears. Centuries of metaphysical thinking have not succeeded, and will never succeed, in curing man of anthropomorphism, in his private thought about Him."[52]

The majority of Christians emerged from the work of Western missionaries in Nigeria. In the early twentieth century these pioneers entered lives in ways that were built on traditional African worldviews. This has put down deep roots into the African traditional religious past and the missionaries' use of the vernacular in the adoption of vernacular names for God and in translation of the Scriptures. This brought recognition that the God the missionaries proclaimed was not an alien import. Africans had a general concept of a supreme being and names of different gods in their languages. However, Romans 1:21–23 explains that the knowledge of God from the gospel is far different from that which is taught and learned from the law. Africans, to some extent, had a knowledge of God from the natural law of creation. But they neither knew him nor glorified him correctly. Missionaries proceeded to adopt local vocabulary to preach the gospel and pointed them to right knowledge of the Triune God. Paul used the symbol dedicated to the "unknown God" to point the Athenian Greeks to God (Acts 17:23, 31). People are created in the image of God. They are singled out for greatness above animals (Ps 8).

50. Adekoya, 8.

51. Parrinder, *West African Religion*, 2.

52. Bolaji, *Olodumare*, 39.

Therefore, Christians' approach to the gospel should not contradict what Scripture teaches. Bebbington believes that "this is central to the believers' faith which is in the life, death and resurrection of Jesus Christ, who is the supreme intervention by God in history."[53] This has implications for the African believer's worldview, whether it is related to the supernatural world, the style and message of the Christian church, or behavior toward the Scripture. This is the simple argument put forward by Kwame Bediako, "Africans face a growing challenge from pluralism and not just a plurality of interests for influence within the bounds of commonly accepted state."[54] Instead, there exists a plurality of loyalties and citizenships and all that implies with each seeking control of a relatively weak central government whose main claim to power is its ability to dispense goods and services.[55] While a large part of the North was so converted, many non-Muslim groups successfully resisted the war, repelled the warriors, and to a large extent embraced Christianity. Most of the groups in the North Central zone fall in this category.[56]

History of Mission Work in Nigeria

Ogbu observes that "the core competition in West Africa is between Christianity and Islam. Islam mixes political power, ethnicity and religion into one overarching unity."[57] In contrast, Christianity developed democratic liberalism and the privatization of faith and its modern secular state.[58] Ogbu further alleges that

> the patterns of the church's responses to the challenges of primal African culture and religion; the theological pretensions of the state; resurgent Islam; and the pluralism created by modernization and global market economy are essential indicators of its capacity to respond to the challenges of power and poverty.[59]

---

53. Bebbington, *Patterns in History*, 142–45.
54. Bediako, *Theology and Identity*, 26.
55. Bediako, 26.
56. Bediako, 26.
57. Kalu, "Jesus Christ," 235–64.
58. Kalu, 252.
59. Kalu, 252.

Indeed, the light of the gospel that gave birth to a flourishing church in North Africa grew dim in the subsequent centuries of Christianity. Although it took many years, the light came once again to Africa, this time to the sub-Saharan countries. Many who walked in darkness came to faith in Christ by accepting the message of salvation. They opened the door and prepared the way for many who followed their footsteps and were responsible for the spread of the gospel in West Africa so the light shone once again.

The first attempt to sow the seed of the gospel in West Africa, especially in Nigeria, was made by Portuguese traders and Catholic missionaries who came to Benin and Warri around the end of the fifteenth century. Their efforts did not bring any lasting results, for which historians give several reasons. Tribal wars and disease, especially malaria made it difficult for Europeans. Thus, Tucker points out, "Black Africa, known for centuries as the white man's graveyard, claimed the lives of more missionaries than any other area of the world."[60] Traditional religion and culture dominated the lives of the people. While a few priests continued to come, they did not make much of an effort to train local catechists who might have provided continuity in the work.[61] Then, the lifestyle and commercial interests of the clergy, often including the slave trade, were contradictory to the teachings of Christianity. Furthermore, there was often political instability.[62] Local rulers were often concerned with expanding and protecting their territories. If they saw that mission work would advance their interests, they welcomed the presence of the priests. But for the most part, these early mission efforts did not see Christianity take root.[63]

By the middle of the nineteenth century, the modern missionary era in Nigeria was under way. It is noted that freed slaves who had become Christians while in different countries played a significant role in taking the gospel back to their home countries in various parts of West Africa. Lamin Sanneh points out that many former slaves returned to their people in the Lagos, Badagry, and Abeokuta areas. Thomas Birch Freeman, a Methodist born in England, the son of an English mother and an African father, who

60. Tucker, *From Jerusalem to Irian Jaya*, 139, 162.

61. Tucker, 162.

62. Sanneh, *Translating the Message*, 35–52, 120–22.

63. Isichei, *History of Christianity in Africa*, 61–73.

spent many years as a missionary in the Asante Kingdom, now called Ghana, came to Lagos Coast on 24 September 1842.[64] During this time he also traveled to Dahomey (Benin) and the Yoruba land in Nigeria to try to establish churches in those lands.[65] Samuel Ajayi Crowther of the Church Missionary Society established a station at Abeokuta. Crowther was one of those who had been "recaptured" while on a slave ship and rescued from slavery.[66] After slavery was abolished, he and many other recaptured slaves were sent to Sierra Leone to live in colonies established for freed slaves.

It was there he became a Christian and was educated.[67] Around 1843, Crowther returned to Nigeria and made a significant contribution that extended beyond preaching the gospel. He wrote a Yoruba grammar, translated many books of the Bible into the Yoruba language, and even produced a primer in the Igbo language.[68] He also published journals describing his expeditions on the Niger River. Walls suggests that Crowther eventually became the first African bishop in West Africa.[69] There is no doubt from this documentation that African slaves contributed much as pioneer missionaries in Nigeria. They and their converts were used by God to open the West Coast of Africa to the gospel. The historian Isichei argues that "the most successful missionaries in the nineteenth and twentieth century West Africa were Africans."[70]

In 1850, the Baptists from America began to send missionaries to this area. By the end of the nineteenth century, the Western missionary movement had made advances, taking the gospel into the interior.[71] New mission societies came to Nigeria seeking ways to penetrate inland from the coast. The Qua Iboe Mission from Ireland sent European missionaries in 1887. Crowther, the Anglican bishop who had died in 1891, had the desire to grow congregations in the north of Nigeria since 1857.[72] He promoted cordial relationships with

64. Sanneh, *Translating the Message*, 120–22.
65. Sanneh, 120–22.
66. Isichei, *History of Christianity in Africa*, 171; and Sanneh, *Translating the Message*, 75.
67. Isichei, *History of Christianity in Africa*, 171; and Sanneh, *Translating the Message*, 75.
68. Walls, *Cross-Cultural Process*, 143–64; see also Walls, *Missionary Movement*, 132–39.
69. Walls, *Cross-Cultural Process*, 139.
70. Isichei, *History of Christianity in Africa*, 156.
71. Isichei, 156.
72. Crampton, *Christianity in Northern Nigeria*, 28–29.

the Northern emirs. But he was not forthright enough for the young radical Church Missionary Society evangelicals.[73] Ayandele notes that "statistics were produced to show that Islam was winning more converts in Africa than all the efforts of Christian missions put together."[74] He further notes that Northern Nigeria was of special romantic and strategic interest for Christian missions.[75] Crampton says, "The Sudan Party eventually truncated the work of Samuel Ajayi Crowther."[76] The missionaries expected very quick results. Brooke had calculated that within six months, much of Northern Nigeria would be converted.[77] Ayandele writes that

> no such large band of missionaries had been dispatched to a single mission field at one time as the Sudan Party; no set of missionaries had been given greater publicity; no Exeter Hall meeting had been more largely attended than the one in which the missionaries were dispatched; no missionaries had excited so much hope as the Sudan Party.[78]

And yet, surprisingly, their resounding failure, rather than being acknowledged, evoked apathy and increased the illusions.[79] In contrast to the unbridled optimism and illusions of the Church Missionary Society and the Sudan Party was the hostile reaction of Northern Nigerians to white people in general, all of whom they regarded as Christians.[80] The records also show that the Muslims had implacable contempt for *kafiris*,[81] as they termed the unbelievers. Ayandele quoted Clapperton saying, "Many Muslims believed that Christians did not have features of human beings."[82] The unmitigated failure of the Sudan Party did not quench the ardor of people who had been led to

73. The advent of a large party of European CMS missionaries was known as the Sudan Party.

74. Ayandele, *Missionary Impact on Modern Nigeria*, 120.

75. Ayandele, 120.

76. Crampton, *Christianity in Northern Nigeria*, 28–29.

77. Ayandele, *Missionary Impact on Modern Nigeria*, 121.

78. Ayandele, 121.

79. Ayandele, 121.

80. Ayandele, 121.

81. Ayandele explains the word meaning "unbelievers." In Hausa language, *kafiris* can also mean those people who are without religion. That is how Muslims perceived non-Muslims generally.

82. Ayandele, *Missionary Impact on Modern Nigeria*, 121.

believe that the Hausas would be the most excellent material for mass conversion to Christianity. In 1892, the leader of the Sudan Party, G.W. Brooke, was afraid of a Muslim uprising.[83] The Sudan United Mission and the Sudan Interior Mission sent missionaries immediately thereafter.[84]

Background of Christianity in Nigeria

The purpose of this section is to provide a brief historical background of the missionaries who planted the Christian church in Nigeria.[85] It examines the early history of Sudan Interior Mission (SIM),[86] which later became the African Industrial Mission and as well as the African Evangelistic Mission.[87] Faught traces the founding missionaries of the Christians.[88]

> In the latter part of the nineteenth century, Christianity seemed literally to be on the march, redrawing its historic Mediterranean and Eurocentric map to include the far-flung territories of the British Empire. North America, India, and the South Pacific all had by now experienced to a greater or lesser degree the impact of the King James Version of the Bible.[89]

"By the 1890s, Africa, too, was a target of the missionary imperative characteristic of earnest late-Victorian Christianity."[90] The Sudan Interior Mission was formed in the 1890s and became the largest Protestant interdenominational mission in Africa.[91] In June 1893, Rowland Bingham met in Toronto with Mrs. Margaret Gowans, a staunch Christian woman with keen missionary instincts for the spiritual needs of the Sudan. "She spread out the vast extent of those thousands of miles south of the Great Sahara," Bingham recounted, "As she told of the sixty to ninety million people without a single missionary, she led me on from the rising waters of the Niger and the great

83. Ayandele, 122.

84. Ayandele, 122.

85. Ayandele, 122.

86. At the emergence of SIM in Africa, much of sub-Saharan Africa was known generally as the "Soudan," which literally means "land of the blacks."

87. Faught, "Missionaries, Indirect Rule," 147–69.

88. Faught, 147–69.

89. Faught, 147.

90. Faught, 147.

91. Tucker, "Rowland Bingham," 295–99.

river Nile. I closed that first interview in her home. She had placed upon me the 'burden of the Sudan.'"[92] Acting on this deep conviction, Bingham and two colleagues, Thomas Kent and Walter Gowans (Mrs. Gowans' son), shipped out for Africa and in December 1893 landed on the Nigerian coast, in Lagos.[93] Walter Gowans wrote in his diary:

> The success in this enterprise means nothing more than the opening of the Sudan for the gospel. Our failure at most, is nothing more than the death of two or three diluted fanatics for the Lord. But if we fail, it will be our fault through lack of faith. God is faithful. He fails not. Still even death is not a failure if God's purposes are accomplished. He was dead as well no life for the furtherance of his cause. After all, is it not worth a venture? Sixty million souls are at stake.[94]

When they landed at the coast of Lagos, they were met with a discouraging message from the superintendent of the Methodist Mission in West Africa, saying, "Young men, you will never see the Sudan, your children will never see the Sudan, your grandchildren may."[95] In 1901, the Sudan Interior Mission missionary pioneers met Lord Lugard, the colonial commander and later High Commissioner, who had set in machinery to conquer Northern Nigeria. Lugard assisted the pioneers in traveling up the River Niger where they started the first mission station at Pategi among the Nupe people.[96] The missionaries introduced themselves to Lugard as leaders of the African Industrial Mission projects as a means of supporting themselves and providing an alternative economic base to society.[97] Barnes argues that up until the late 1920s colonial officials opposed most missionaries for several reasons, among which were the following: (1) they objected to the impacts of evangelism; (2) most missionaries were considered as ill-educated, unprofessional, unsuccessful, and

92. Hunter, *Flame of Fire*, 55.

93. Hunter, 55.

94. Bingham, *Seven Sevens and a Jubilee*, 55.

95. There is the need to further explain Sudan at that time. "The great area south of the Sahara between the Niger and Nile Rivers which was then called the Sudan."

96. Bingham, *Seven Sevens and a Jubilee*, 31–32.

97. Bingham, 31–32.

the Americans among them were viewed as fundamentalists and fanatical;[98] (3) they lacked social graces, common sense, self-discipline, and they had entirely different goals leading to conflicts between the missionaries and the British governments.[99] Ubah observes that Lord Lugard used the Islamic government institution to extend Islamic rule over non-Muslim areas.[100] Walls describes how a missionary in Northern Nigeria, W. R. S. Millar, complained that the British government did not practice neutrality in religion. "Were the government truly neutral, Islam would not be making the progress it was in Nigeria, where the Plateau people had long experience of harsh treatment from Muslims. But while Muslim missionaries were allowed to go anywhere under British administration, Christian missionaries were restricted".[101]

Missionaries' Restrictions

Stanley argues, "British colonial policy in Northern Nigeria seemed actively in favor of Islam to advance the cause of Islam instead of the Gospel of Christ."[102] Isichei says, "One of the most harmful legacies of Colonialism in West Africa was its invention of North and South. The Muslim North was to be isolated from disruptive forces of modernity and from Christian missions."[103] Those who went to Hausa land hoping for spontaneous turning away from Islam were soon disappointed.[104] The expectation that the Hausas would rise against the Fulani and that the whole Hausa world was waiting for Christ proved groundless, and missionary access to the North was rigidly restricted by British officials who often seemed more hostile to Western influences than the emirs themselves.[105]

As the largest missionary society in Northern Nigeria, Sudan Interior Mission was intimately involved in the struggle with the colonial authorities for entrance into the Muslim emirates. Relationships with the colonial government remained difficult. Missionaries were forbidden to preach in market

98. Barnes, "'Evangelization Where It Was Not Wanted," 412–413.
99. Crampton, *Christianity in Northern Nigeria*, 59–60.
100. Ubah, "Colonial Administration," 133.
101. Walls, *Cross-Cultural Process*, 151.
102. Stanley, *Bible and Flag*, 135.
103. Isichei, *History of Christianity in Africa*, 273.
104. Isichei, 273.
105. Isichei, 273.

places or near mosques. They were not allowed to do house-to-house visitation. Beacham points out that "agitation to prohibit the teaching of children under eighteen of Muslim parents whether or not the parents desire their children to attend a Christian school or church service has been a hindrance to advancement of the gospel in some places."[106] Olatayo refers to a 1951 plea by the Emir of Gwandu not to proselytize sixteen school children with leprosy: "That such a plea was made more than ten years after the matter was first raised suggests that the freedom of missionaries had not been effectively circumscribed."[107]

Despite restrictions and discrimination against the missionaries, Sudan Interior Mission planted the Evangelical Church Winning All (ECWA).[108] The church has grown in numbers since it was incorporated in a 1954 registration by the Federal Government of Nigeria with a membership of over six million.[109] The absence of religious freedom continued, even after ECWA was formed in 1954[110] into one indigenous, self-supporting, self-governing, and self-propagating, corporate organization, legally recognized by the Nigerian government. This was to allow it to inherit the property of the planting missionaries and continue the work in case the mission was ever expelled from Nigeria.[111] Fuller made reference to Ray Davis saying that the new ECWA church faced impossible odds. "History and culture were against her. One of those opponents was Islam, and its discrimination against Christians and traditionalists."[112] The absence of religious freedom concerned delegates attending the 1956 church general assembly. The inclusion of a human rights clause in the Federal Constitution would provide legal safeguards. Sir Ahmadu Bello, the Northern Region's Premier, was invited to address a joint ECWA/SIM meeting in Jos.

The Premier reassured all concerned that there would be no interference in mission work although Muslims would not be encouraged to convert to

106. Olatayo, *ECWA: Book 1*, 13.

107. Olatayo, 39.

108. Olatayo, 40–41.

109. Musa, Danladi, ECWA *Strategic Plan 2007–216*, Jos, Nigeria: Challenge Press,2007,1.

110. Olatayo, *ECWA: Book 1*, 1–48.

111. Olatayo, 21.

112. Fuller, *Mission-Church Dynamics*, 199.

Christianity.[113] Churches were concerned about the religious and political freedom of their new converts in Northern Nigeria. The situation compelled the Anglican, TEKAN, and other church denominations to produce a joint statement to the Willinks' commission hearing in Zaria,[114] calling for guarantees of fair representation, equality under the law, religious liberty, and equal rights to education, employment, and promotion.[115] These church denominations did not make any representation regarding a state creation; rather, they sought constitutional guarantees.[116] Olatayo affirms that these requests were granted in 1959 when a Human Rights Declaration for the Northern Region was promulgated.[117] However, independence came on 1 October 1960. Missionaries became extremely apprehensive of the changes. Kastfelt notes that "Danish Lutherans and their converts in Numan and Yola observed the moods of missionaries were very uncertain. Various questions were raised. What would happen with their schools and mission stations? How would it face the challenges of nationalism and Islam?"[118] For example, to meet these challenges, the Danish Lutheran missionaries redoubled their evangelism, developed their leadership training for church purposes and secular leaders the country would need in the path of church self-government.[119] There were reported cases of violence against Christians and denial of human rights, "as a body and as individuals, members were denied rights which were granted to other citizens: rights to parcels of land to locate and build church property and buildings respectively; denied freedom of proclamation of one's faith and so forth."[120] The meeting also heard reports of an anonymous political leader's threat to burn a church, in a particular village, if it held services while he campaigned there. Sir Ahmadu Bello could not get to the village, as "God

113. Olatayo, *ECWA: Book 1*, 39–41.

114. Bagudu N., ed. *Proceedings at the Sir Henry Willinks Commission Appointed to Enquire into the Fears of the Minorities and Means of Allaying Them*, Volume 1 (Jos: League for Human Rights, 2003), 220–38.

115. Bagudu, *Proceedings at the Sir Henry Willinks Commission Appointed to Enquire into the Fears of the Minorities and Means of Allaying Them*, 220–38.

116. Bagudu, *Proceedings at the Sir Henry Willinks Commission Appointed to Enquire into the Fears of the Minorities and Means of Allaying Them*, 220–38.

117. Olatayo, *ECWA: Book 1*, 42–43.

118. Kastfelt, *Religion and Politics in Nigeria*, 36–38.

119. Kastfelt, 38.

120. Olatayo, *ECWA: Book 2*, 33–34, 53, 55.

intervened by sending out fire from His presence, the fire burnt up his car on the way to the village."[121] Loves notes, "This new impetus to spread Islam by Ahmadu Bello, the Premier of Northern Region after Nigerian independence in 1960 that led to the conversion of over 100,000 people in the provinces of Zaria and Niger."[122]

In the 1970s government policy continued to favor the long dominance of Islam in Northern Nigeria as is evidenced in today's sharia states.[123]

Background of Northern Nigeria

Early Hausa States

Anthony points out that the best evidence of early civilization in Northern Nigeria is provided by the Nok terracotta heads, which are named after a village of the Jaba people, Kwoi, in Northern Nigeria.[124] Important among the groups that established some of the largest Northern regions and most enduring were the Hausa states during the first millennium BC.[125] The economy and the culture of the early Hausa states were deeply shaped by trade. They were village-dwelling cultivators, artisans, weavers, dyers, smiths, and leather workers who produced goods for local markets as well as long distance caravans living on the belt of the open woodland and grass Savanna known as the Sahel, on the Southern edge of the Sahara.[126] From the southern forested regions, these caravans brought ivory, gold, and slaves. From the north, they brought desert salt and other goods from the Mediterranean area, since around the ninth century.[127] After about 1000 BC, the rise of Hausa statehood coincided with the building of walled cities known as "birane."[128] The kings who resided within the cities were charged with warding off external aggression in return for which they collected taxes from commoners.[129] It was only after

121. Olatayo, 33–34, 53 ,55.

122. Loves, *Beginning of the End*, 201.

123. Loves, 103. He lists the twelve sharia states: Sokoto, Zamfara, Katsina, Kano, Jigawa, Yobe, Borno, Kebbi, Niger, Kaduna, Bauchi, and Gombe.

124. Gates and Appiah, *Africana*, 1432.

125. Gates and Appiah, 1432.

126. Gates and Appiah, 1432.

127. Gates and Appiah, 1432.

128. "Birane" in the Hausa language means "cities" in English.

129. Gates and Appiah, *Africana*, 1432.

the thirteenth century that the Hausa rulers began to convert to Islam and, in the centuries following, cities such as Kano and Katsina became centers for Islamic scholarship as well as commerce.[130] Many Hausa commoners were little affected by Islamic culture until the early nineteenth century when jihad, or crusade, led by the Fulani cleric Usman Dan Fodio created a vast Islamic empire with its headquarters in Sokoto.[131]

Hausa States Conquered

Oyewole gives a brief background about how the

> Hausa states were conquered. Triggered in 1804 by the attempts of King Yunfa of Gobir to stem the cleric's popularity, the Jihad defeated most of the Hausa kings by 1810, putting Usman Dan Fodio and later his own son Mohammad Bello in control of the largest state [now Northern Nigeria] during the nineteenth century, spanning some 400,000 square kilometers (154,440 square miles).[132]

"Dan Fodio installed Muslim Fulani emirs in all the cities he conquered in Northern Nigeria, with the exception of southern Kaduna, Jos, Plateau, and Benue states, which were not conquered."[133]

Sundita believes that "religious people [like Usman Dan Fodio] sought to establish the path to the origins of their belief [Islam] as a 'revival or fundamentalism.'"[134] Sundita is of the belief that they did this with the hope of connecting to the source of their ideology, arguing,

> Whenever Muslims retrace their path to Muhammad, the result has always been to pick up the sword against the infidel because Islam prospered on violence and therefore will never go past that. . . . The actions of Muhammad and his immediate followers clearly demonstrate that unprovoked violence, terror,

130. Gates and Appiah, 1432.
131. Gates and Appiah, *Africana*, 1433.
132. Oyewole, 143.
133. Oyewole, 144.
134. Sundita, *Look Behind the Facade*, 15.

> intolerance, deceit, murder, hypocrisy, and pillage continually were employed as instruments of control.[135]

The Northern Empire under Islamic control lasted for one hundred years and in 1903, Lord Lugard conquered the empire and brought it under the British High Commission.[136] Thus, the north came under colonial rule.[137] The north, east, and west emerged as a result of colonial policy and the British retained the pre-colonial Hausa-Fulani Muslim feudal rulers of the north. The British allowed them to extend their rule over the peoples of the Middle Belt, few of whom were Muslims at that time.[138] Colonial powers were far more interested in economic endeavors than religious conversion and they created roadblocks to limit the work of Christian missionaries.[139] Miller argues, "While Muslim missionaries were allowed to go anywhere under the British administration, Christian missionaries were restricted."[140] Thus, Faught argues that the emirs of Northern Nigeria were very interested in Lord Lugard and his policy of religious neutrality, which was decreed to promote their sustained cooperation.[141] Crampton critically maintains that fears of religious violence and discrimination in the North by the Muslim majority were referred to several times by Christians.[142]

Gofwen argues that "since independence in 1960, Nigeria has continued to grapple with the task and challenges of nation building."[143] Gofwen believes that "given her pre-colonial and colonial experiences, the challenges have in fact been daunting. The welfare of composite ethnic and religious groups within depends on the realization of the goal of nation building."[144] Religious conflicts, frequently involving violence, death, and destruction have been witnessed in the country. According to Gofwen, "The nation has been threatened as religious conflicts continue to undermine requisite security, and political

135. Sundita, 15.
136. Oyewole, *Historical Dictionary of Nigeria*, 148–73.
137. Oyewole, 148–173.
138. Johnstone and Mandryk, *Operation World*, 493.
139. Jacobsen, *World's Christians*, 161.
140. Walls, *Cross-Cultural Process*, 151.
141. Faught, "Missionaries, Indirect Rule," 160.
142. Crampton, *Christianity in Northern Nigeria*, 84.
143. Gofwen, *Religious Conflicts in Northern Nigeria*, 1.
144. Gofwen, 1.

stability, economic development, good and democratic governance as well as protection of human rights."[145] Gofwen summarizes Nigeria's threat that the transition from colonial to neo-colonial state of independence saddled the post-colonial states with the task of transforming the inherited states beyond the level of mere geographical entities held together by repression. He argues that "instead of providing a united force against neo-colonialism, states became bedeviled with ethnic and religious problems and most of *these resulted in various fratricidal wars, which have threatened the existence of most African states, past and present*."[146]

Osaghae and Suberu argue that "Nigeria can rightly be described as one of the most deeply divided states in Africa."[147] Between 1980 and the present day, different instances of religiously related violence have continued to occur in Northern Nigeria. Each phenomenon builds on the unresolved issues of previous outbreaks resulting in the deaths of thousands.[148] Repeatedly churches, mosques, hotels, shops, petrol stations, individual's homes, and personal lives have been destroyed causing tremendous financial hardship on the usually uninsured owners.[149] Many have been injured, and hundreds more carry emotional scars, scars that hardly heal as almost annually another round of bloodshed results in fresh losses. Since then, religious violence between Muslims and Christians has characterized Northern Nigeria.

For example, a group of Muslims took upon themselves the duty of stopping cars along major roads and forcing their passengers to recite the *Shahada* Islamic creed.[150] Those who could do so were allowed to pass. If passengers were unable to recite the creed, they were beaten and killed. Given the religious climate in Nigeria, many Christians were involved and their inability or refusal to recite the *Shahada* precipitated many beatings and deaths. In

145. Gofwen, 1.

146. Examples are: Zaire in 1960; Sudan, Nigeria, Rwanda and Burundi in the 1970s and 1980s; Chad, Uganda, Ethiopia and Sudan in the 1990s; and Liberia, Somalia, Ethiopia, Sierra Leone, and Equatorial Guinea among others. Gofwen, 1.

147. Osaghae and Suberu, *History of Identities*, 4.

148. Gofwen, *Religious Conflicts in Northern Nigeria*, 1, 82–119.

149. Gofwen, 88.

150. The *Shahada* is an Arabic version of Muslim profession of faith. "There is no god but Allah, and Mohammed is the prophet of Allah." The *Shahada* is the first of the five pillars of Islam. It must be recited by every Muslim at least once in a lifetime, aloud correctly and purposively with a full understanding of its meaning and with an assent of heart.

response, the Christians in the same way stopped cars and forced passengers to recite portions of Scripture, for example, John 1:12 or John 3:16.[151] Those passengers, who were unable to recite Scripture were beaten or killed.[152]

The principle of an "eye for an eye" appears to be an ongoing method of responding to violence as Nigerian Christians abandon "cheek-turning," with no more cheeks to turn.[153] A fringe Christian militia emerged vowing to match blood for more blood and some pastors' approval of the self-defense response to violence has spiraled into angrier retaliation that has continued to fuel revenge and death over the past twenty-five years.[154] Today, religion in modern Nigeria is divided between a Christian culture and a radical Islamic culture. Christians who advocated for pacifism speak of "no more cheeks left to turn."[155] Oguntola believes that the shift from pacifism toward self-defense developed as a result of the Kafanchan and Kaduna religious violence, which began in March 1980. He notes that Christians in central Nigeria and in Northern cities mobilized to defend themselves, organizing vigilante groups to respond to Muslim attacks.[156] Philemon asks, "What is the central intellectual heresy that values death over life and allows the Muslim provocative to turn into killers in the name of religion or God?"[157] The church in Africa has to develop an understanding of the nature of violence and how Christians are to respond to them. This is a problem that the church needs to address if the church wants to continue to be salt and light of the world in which she lives as a witness (Matt 5:16).

151. See also the account of Jan H. Boer, *Nigeria's Decades of Blood*. Boer Lived and taught in Jos, Plateau State, Central Nigeria for many years before returning to Europe.

152. Obed Minchakpu is an independent journalist, who previously served as the editor of *Today's Challenge*. See Minchakpu, "Eye for an Eye," 17. Nyberg, "Pastors Killed, Churches Burned," 17.

153. Oguntola, "No More Cheeks to Turn," 14.

154. Oguntola, 14.

155. Oguntola, 14.

156. Oguntola, 14.

157. Gideon Philemon and the researcher traveled from Kaduna back to Jos in February 2001 during one of the incidents of major violence. Muslim youth went on a rampage, and mounted a road block. Both men narrowly escaped death.

Purpose of the Research

The purpose of this research is to examine why some Christians in Northern Nigeria have resorted to violent means in response to religious violence. The researcher wants to drive the point home to Christians that God is the author of life (Gen 1:1; 2:7). The researcher wants Christians to understand that anything that God creates should not be thoughtlessly destroyed. As Christians, they are to play the role of saving, preserving, and restoring life instead of destroying life.

The violence that African Christianity is suffering has great implications for the church – just as Walls points out that "Christianity remains vulnerable and even those areas seen as the heartlands of Christianity are capable of retreat and even extinction."[158] The church in Africa has to develop an understanding of the nature of this violence and how Christians are to respond to it. This is a problem that the church needs to address if the church wants to continue to be salt and light of the world we live in (Matt 5:13–16). The researcher also wants Christians to see Christ as the Savior of the whole universe through whom the world exists (Col 1:16), so that they will come to realize that no experience in which they find themselves is outside the power and knowledge of God (2 Tim 3:12). Jesus Christ who lives in them is greater than the world's spiritual forces that cause trouble (John 16:33).

This research seeks to offer to Christians in general the right approach when responding to religious violence in Northern Nigeria. The research is not only for the researcher to accomplish his missiological academic requirements for a degree, but also, more importantly, to help Christians in general know how to face and respond to the challenges religious violence has posed to Christianity, in Northern Nigeria, Africa, and elsewhere in the world.

Rationale for the Research Problem

The rationale to research this particular area on religious violence has burdened the researcher for many years, having served the Lord for over thirty years in pastoral theological education and in leadership roles at both national and international levels around sub-Saharan African churches, and as a result

158. Walls, *Cross-Cultural Process*, 27–48.

of the researcher's own love for God and his church. Prior to commencing this research, the researcher lived all of his life in Northern and Central Nigeria. The researcher himself narrowly escaped death during some of the bloody Muslim provocative violence that has continued unabated in Northern Nigeria for several decades.[159] Shedrack notes that, "For nearly forty years the northern ruling elite gave preferential treatment to Muslims and discriminated against Christians. There have been upsurges in the occurrences of religious violence across Northern Nigeria."[160]

The researcher has been pondering why Christians in Northern Nigeria have resorted to violence in response to religious violence. Through many years of serving the Lord in pastoral theological education and leadership roles at both national and international levels in the sub-Saharan African church, the researcher has watched the church in Northern Nigeria with growing concern. This burden is in agreement with Booth that a researcher should have missiological concern and interest in the project chosen.[161] At the initial stage of religious violence, Christians in Northern Nigeria appeared to have taken pacifist positions in promoting peaceful and prayerful responses to religious violence. This is on the basis of what Abashiya and Ulea have written about those days of pacifism. They write, "If you are forty years or above in age you may begin to wonder what on earth has gone wrong with religious people of Nigeria?"[162]

The researcher watched deteriorating relationships between Christians and Muslims and since then desired peaceful restoration. This project therefore, is an expression of the researcher's desire to help not only the Northern Nigerian people, but an expression of love that contributes to the concern of global missiology as the work would be helpful to the general body of believers everywhere. After spending many fruitful years of ministry in sub-Saharan African countries, especially Northern Nigeria, and around Africa, his desire for such a research project kept growing as he served churches in contemporary Africa and in Nigeria.

159. Boer, *Nigeria's Decades of Blood*, 34.

160. Best, *Conflicts and Peace Building*, 3.

161. Booth, Colomb, and Williams, *Craft of Research*, 40–45.

162. Abashiya and Ulea, *Christianity and Islam*, 1.

The researcher, like any other mature Christian leader, has struggled with the problem of religious violence and its hindrances to the peaceful existence in the environment. It is a praise-worthy experience for him to observe that most of the church members exhibited endurance and restraint in the midst of religious violence for dying in Christ because of their faith in him. Their examples have caused others not to renounce their faith but live victoriously in the midst of serious religious violence.

However, there is still the need for the church to learn to listen to the cries and the crises of violence affecting Christians who are discouraged so that the church may have insight to respond appropriately. There is nothing as disheartening for the researcher, himself a leader, as seeing members of his congregation experiencing and struggling in the midst of religious violence because of their faith. This has caused spiritual disaster for many congregations and is also a concern for the church leadership. He also observed that religious violence in Northern Nigeria has increased over the years. His interactions with Christians in Northern Nigeria, since the 1980s during many years of ministry, and with the students he taught in seminary in Jos, Nigeria, have confirmed that congregations in Northern Nigeria are living in the face of religious violence that tends to leave them confused in how they are to respond to religious violence. The researcher also knows that church history teaches that the blood of those who died in religious violence for their faith is not always the seed of the church but may rather spell its decline and the demise of congregational membership.

For this reason, this area of study has been prayerfully selected with the hope that possible principles or guidelines identified might come to bear and be helpful to members, pastors, and missionaries who serve in the field. It is the researcher's desire that principles and recommendations adopted in the course of this research will help Christians in Northern Nigeria and elsewhere to stand firm and remain faithful to Christ when experiencing religious violence. The Catholic church, as an example of other churches in Northern Nigeria, is also faced with the problem of violence in the north. In his book, *The Christian Churches and the Democratization of Africa*, edited by Paul Gifford, the Catholic Bishop Matthew Hassan Kukah writes, "The burning of churches in the city of Kano in October 1982 which led to intolerance in the corridors of Christianity encouraged many Christians to take too far a more militant approach toward arresting this unfortunate trend, thus exacerbating tension."[163] It is undeniable that the experience of the Anglican Bishop is not an isolated occurrence. Many African and Nigerian church leaders share the same burdens and apprehension.[164]

Religious Violence

Hebrew has two words for violence: *khamas* and *shodh*. In English this word carries the meaning, "physical force so as to injure, damage, roughness in action and negatively as the use of force, or power, as in deprivation of rights, and brute strength that inflicts pain, injury, cruel or unjust action, with hostile intent."[165] The term *khamas* conveys the meaning "to oppress, or to afflict."[166] Thus, violence cannot occur unless the perpetrator actually acts out their violent inclinations. This action must be perceived as unjust and reveals itself in diverse ways. If this happens, violence occurs within a broader spectrum, and ranges from unjust actions that are intensely hostile to those that are mildly hostile. Intensely hostile actions can be executed physically, psychologically, and socially. These could encompass actions such as beating, discrimination, torture, and even death. Such an action usually strikes at an individual's basic needs. For instance, a pastor from the northeast of Nigeria denied the presence of religious violence because he personally saw no cases of physical brutality even though his church, under a religiously oppressive governor, was denied access to worship. The governor demolished many worship places in the district church of that chairman.

It is well known that in parts of Jos North and South in Central Nigeria, worshippers traveled to church using complex and varying routes in order to avoid confrontation and potentially death. Schlossberg maintains that similar responses are common among Christians in other regions of the world, including areas where religious freedom may be the law, but in practice Christians are still subject to a wide range of violence.[167] The *Merriam-Webster Collegiate Dictionary* states that violence results in "bodily harm," or

163. Kukah, "Christians and Nigeria's Aborted Transition," 225.

164. Kukah, 225.

165. Agnes, *Webster's New World College Dictionary*, 1595.

166. Middleton, *New Interpreter's Dictionary of the Bible*, 783.

167. Schlossberg, *Called to Suffer*, 17.

"oppress cruelly," especially due to religion, politics or violence.[168] However, the definition of violence by Barrett, Kurian, and Johnson underscores a theological meaning of religious violence toward Christians. These authors write that violence is "any unjust action of varying levels of hostility perpetrated primarily on the basis of religion and directed at Christians resulting in varying levels of harm as it is considered from the victim's perspective."[169] This meaning of religious violence has three important elements, which can further be elucidated as follows.

1. Varying levels of hostility/varying levels of harm. Religious violence manifests itself within a broad spectrum ranging from mildly hostile to intensely hostile actions. Mildly hostile actions are less intense and can be carried out psychologically or socially. These actions can include ridicule, restriction, certain kinds of harassment, or discrimination. Intensely hostile actions lie at the opposite end of the spectrum and can also be carried out psychologically or socially, as well as physically. In the light of this, one cannot theologically define religious violence based on the level of harm it might cause or level of hostility in which it occurs. Rather, it must be understood to encompass actions spanning the full range of hostility, from mild to intense.
2. Perpetrated primarily on the basis of religion. Religious violence often occurs with an overlap of motivations, for example religion, race, culture, politics, and so forth. Religious violence occurs when religion is the primary factor involved in the event. With this in mind, Marshall provides the helpful demarcation that

   > if the persons had other religious beliefs, would they still be treated in the same way? If the answer is yes, we probably should not call it specifically religious violence, though not for a second should we forget that it is real violence and that it is real people who suffer.[170]

168. *Merriam-Webster's Collegiate Dictionary,* Tenth Edition (Springfield: Merriam-Webster Incorporated, 1998), s.v. "Violence".

169. Barrett, Kurian, and Johnson, *World Christian Encyclopedia*, 27.

170. Marshall, "Persecution of Christians," 2–8.

3. The victim's perspective. Perhaps most important, this aspect acknowledges the fact that violent people cannot be the judges of their actions. For example, in the early parts of Acts, we see Saul violently arresting and murdering followers of Jesus Christ, because to Saul they posed a threat to the Jewish religious system. Saul's actions were surely justifiable to him in light of how he viewed Christians and their claims. In Acts 9:1–6, however, Jesus himself clarifies this issue for Saul saying that not only is he violating the church, but he is doing violence to Christ himself. From the perspective of Saul's victims his actions were unjust and violent.

Koschorke argues that when there is a situation where restrictions and violent actions against a particular religious belief are widespread and consistent, such actions are to be classified "as religious harassment and religious discrimination."[171] It is, therefore, important to distinguish religious violence from sociopolitical violence. Sociopolitical definitions in general understand religious violence to be any systematic violence of religious freedom.[172] Although the word "religious" is not readily available in the Bible motif, the concept and motif is implied throughout the biblical narrative running through the Old and New Testaments.

Research Concern Over Time

The subject of violence permeates the writings of both the Old and New Testaments, and is a general phenomenon in the history of humanity. The issue of violence runs through the times of the Maccabees; the Zealots believed there was no contradiction between prayer and the sword. It is surprising to observe that violence and destruction have been part and parcel of religions even back to biblical times. Why does religion seem to need violence and why is a divine mandate for destruction accepted with such certainty by some believers?[173] Divine mandate for destruction goes back to the Old Testament

171. Koschorke, Ludwig, and Delgado, *Christianity in Asia, Africa and Latin America*, 268.
172. Marshall, "Persecution of Christians," 19–30.
173. Huntington, *Clash of Civilizations*, 252.

(Deuteronomy 7 and Joshua 6; 7, and 8), and is also found among other nations in the Ancient Near East. In Africa today the subject of war is seldom international. Rather, war tends to involve two or more religious groups, which means that in African thought it contains more religious violence. In more recent times, Muslim faiths have come under the spotlight because of renewed religious conflicts. This has not spared Africa either. The sub-Saharan churches have been characterized by violence of all sorts, among these have been religious wars. In Northern Nigeria, there has been a long struggle of religious violence among followers of Islam and Christianity.

Brief Picture of the Research Design and Method

The pilot studies conducted convinced the researcher that the topic was worthy of investigating from the responses of thirty randomly selected participants. The interviews proved positive results from the interaction. The responses revealed that the participants understood what the researcher was examining. The participants' responses were related to the questions the researcher asked. They generally agreed that religious violence had become a menace to Christians in Northern Nigeria. In carrying out this study, there is the need to give some consideration to the methods used and the fundamental presuppositions behind the methods. In researching a particular problem, there are several methods of going about conducting research. However, there are two primary methodologies a researcher could consider and choose from: qualitative and quantitative research methods. Gall suggests that "if a social science field research methodology is proposed, pilot studies are used to refine specific portions or elements of larger, subsequent research phases."[174] It appears to the researcher that some of the participants were timid in the sense that the responses he got from the experiment of the studies expressed fear. The interviewees appeared confused about their Christian worldview with regards to how they respond to violence compared to the teaching of Jesus to love their enemies. For instance, twenty-two of the participants felt that a nonviolent approach in response to religious violence does not bring it to an end.

174. Borg, Gall, and Gall, *Educational Research*, 77.

According to their perspectives, "violence for violence" was the approach that could stop church members from experiencing and suffering in the face of religious violence. Their own philosophical method of responding to religious violence suggested fighting back in self-defense and to defend fellow Christians and churches from being hurt or destroyed. The researcher decided to use the historical qualitative method because he felt the research topic required it. The research requires a historically qualitative method to examine the subject and to deal with why some Christians have resorted to violent means in response to religious violence in Northern Nigeria. Thus, there is the need to examine why they have resorted to violence contrary to the teaching of Jesus Christ in the Bible. Northern Nigeria imposes severe restrictions on non-Muslims. These restrictions are widespread and consistent and therefore should be treated and understood as religious violence. Such explanations provide a specific measurable dichotomy in which Christians' response to religious violence can be examined. In the final run, Christians may be able to differentiate religious violence from political crises to help them respond to religious violence and remain focused and stand firm in their faith. The qualitative research was able to help the researcher to have a direct contact with participants' respondents who shared their personal stories.

The researcher conducted these pilot interviews in Northern Nigeria and Plateau in the central state using English and Hausa languages among the Christians in Northern Nigeria over a period of time between February and December 2001 and fifty-four more interviews with participants from June to December 2013.

Statement of the Research Questions

The purpose of this research is to develop a clearer understanding of the nature of religious violence in Northern Nigeria. The research seeks to examine why some Christians in Northern Nigeria have resorted to violent means in response to religious violence and how the challenges relate to their Christian faith. To assist the researcher in carrying out this research, he has designed some questions to guide him.

1. What was the social and religious context in which the church in Northern Nigeria was planted?

2. How do Christians in Northern Nigeria describe what the Christian message means to them?
3. How do Christians in Northern Nigeria describe the cause of religious violence?
4. What solution(s) to the problem of religious violence do the Christians in Northern Nigeria propose?

Introduction to the Literature

Theologians, philosophers, and Christian ethical writers and their contributions provide insights to the researcher on the subject of religious violence. Arnett explains that "human beings can be violated without their lives being taken by another. Violence is not something that happens only at gun point. It is present whenever the human dignity of an individual is oppressed, ignored or abused."[175] Wink has written that "violence is the ethos of our times. It is the spirituality of the modern world. It has been accorded the status of a religion, demanding from its devotees and absolute obedience to death."[176]

Agreeing that there is a good deal of evidence to support this judgment, Kassmann maintains, "There also seems to be a growing awareness that our world desperately needs a counter ethos that affirms life in order to create livable conditions for generations to come."[177] Windass compares pacifistic early Christianity to mid-twentieth-century Christianity and decides that it was in accordance with Christian principles not only to respond to violence violently in defense, but also by wiping out those who caused violence.[178] Cahill differs and says, "The ultimate consideration in Christian social ethics, when mortal violence is in question, is whether a preferential option is being made for justice for those least able to advance their own cause."[179]

Hauerwas puts forward the question, "How can the church be at this time a people of patience who take the time to step back in the face of terrible events?" He answers, "Christians are a community shaped by the practice of baptism that reminds us there are far worse things that can happen to us than

175. Arnett, *Dwell in Peace*, 13.

176. Wink, *Engaging the Powers*, 15.

177. Kassmann, *Overcoming Violence*, 2.

178. Windass, *Christianity Versus Violence*, 22–24.

179. Cahill, "Danger of Violence," 230.

dying."[180] Sider believes that "God has not suspended the Biblical commands to work for the good of all (Galatians 6:10) and love your enemies (Matthew 5:44). It is crucial that the church offer a Biblical answer to the question."[181] Clapsis wonders "what should be the relationship of the Christian faith to the violence existing in the world and how Christians would respond to violence in a matter that is rooted in faith and their relationship to God?"[182] Hengel believes that "Jesus's liberating message of love without restriction includes also renunciation of violence that destroys one's fellow man physically or mentally."[183] Hengel concludes that "violence has irreparable consequences for the individual and for society."[184]

These writers and many others provide perspectives on religious violence and some of these scholars have offered suggestions concerning how to respond to the question of religious violence as it impacts Christianity. This research examines why some Christians in Northern Nigeria have resorted to violent means in response to religious violence. The attempt shall be made to find out some possible principles in responding to the problem. These scholars are in harmony in that they perceive religious violence as a problem to Christianity, but the views of Hauerwas and Sider are more biblical in their approaches regarding the matter.

180. Hauerwas, "Christian Nonviolence," 246.

181. Sider, "How Should Christians Respond?," 326.

182. Clapsis, *Violence and Christian Spirituality*, 3.

183. Hengel, *Victory Over Violence*, 65.

184. Hengel, 65.

CHAPTER TWO

Biblical Literature and Luther's Works

Old Testament Literature

The moment conflicts start, it is often very easy to resort to violence in an effort to solve it. From the earliest times this has been the case. This researcher begins with the problem of violence from the perspective of the Old Testament because in it we read of violence from almost the very start of human history. The researcher chose two examples of human violence from the Pentateuch, in Genesis 4:6–10 and 6:6–7; another from Psalm 10:15, 17–18, which shows human attitudes towards violence; and finally, three prophetic anticipations of peace ending violence, from Isaiah 4:2, Micah 4:3, and Joel 3:9–10.

Human Violence (Gen 4:6–10; 6:6–7)

A person does not have to read very far into the biblical narrative to find the first heinous act of violence. It describes the action of Cain against his brother Abel. God favored Abel's sacrifice. God did not pay attention to Cain's offering (Gen 4:3–5). Abel's offering was not inherently superior to Cain's offering. Throughout the Old Testament, God looks with favor on offering of grain and other produce, just as he does on offerings of animals (Lev 1–6). God regarded Abel's offering because it was given in true faith (Heb 11:4). Cain made the common mistake of thinking that God can be influenced by means of our offerings (Gen 4:6). God repeatedly reminds his people that he will be gracious to whom he will be gracious, and he will show mercy to whom he will show mercy (Exod 33:19).

In the second generation of humanity, a brother spills the blood of his brother. Cain murders Abel for a reason that comes right from the heart of jealousy. The pattern is set. Jealousy is left unchecked. It is left to grow, deepen, and intensify, and it leads to violence. But those who give in to violence find sin crouching at the door, but "you must rule over it" (Gen 4:6, 7).[1] Cain did not heed God's warning. He gave in to the domination of sin and exercised his angry desire by killing his brother (Gen 4:8). The Bible states that jealousy leads to anger and that sin is predatory, crouching at the door, looking to possess Cain. Violence, in other words, is often the tipping point after resentment turns to rage.

What can be done about violence? God instructed Cain he should "rule over it," the pathology of his soul. He did not heed the warning and instruction, and blood was spilled. God responds to Cain, "The voice of your brother's blood is crying to me from the ground" (Gen 4:8). McEntire writes that this first act of violence foreshadows the wickedness and evil of all humanity and would cause God to blot it out with the flood (Gen 6:5–7).[2] And so does the blood of many today. The first lesson on violence to learn from this biblical passage is that violence is the result of pathology of the soul. Violence does not begin with being with the military, generational tribal hatred, or long-standing social inequities. Rather, violence is as close to us as our own hearts. Later in Genesis a profound principle is laid down regarding the moral depravity of violence. "Whoever sheds the blood of man by man shall his blood be shed, for God made man in his own image" (Gen 9:6 ESV). This is also early in the biblical account. This is foundational in the sense that its links to the fundamental reality that violence against human beings is wrong because human beings were made in the image and likeness of God (Gen 1:26, 27). There is worth and dignity in human life that should not be taken by another person.

Worth and Dignity of Human Life

There is a worth, a value, and a dignity to every human life. This understanding comes from the key Hebrew word used to describe the state of life people

1. Engelbrecht, *Lutheran Study Bible*. All quotations hereafter shall be from this translation, except as otherwise noted.

2. McEntire, *Blood of Abel*, 1.

had originally: "shalom." The word "shalom" portrays "peace, completeness, soundness, and wholeness."[3] The meaning of shalom is further associated with health, prosperity, well-being, security, and as well as quiet from war (Eccl 3:8; Isa 45:7). Shalom is a condition of freedom from strife, whether internal or external security from outward enemies (Isa 26:12), as well of calmness of heart for those trusting God (Job 22:21; Isa 26:3).

In the *Concordia Self-Study Bible*, Roehrs points out, "Man's unique status among all other creatures derives from his relationship to the Creator. It is not a physical replica of God (Isaiah 40:18; Luke 24:39; John 4:24) nor an emanation or a part of God; not independent of God."[4] People are given features that correspond and relate to the Creator. These include the capacity to share in his rulership and responsibility to exercise partnership in a communion with him, reflecting how God wants people to be and act. This bears his "likeness and imprint."[5] When people subsequently broke this divinely stipulated relationship, dragging all creation with them into frustrating disharmony (Rom 8:20–23), they lost the ability to live and act in harmony with God and his fellow human beings as they were intended to do (Gen 3; 5:1–3; Jas 3:9).[6] Capon makes some observations in his book *Is God a Moral Monster?* He lists the following four observations: (1) not everything that happened in the Old Testament times was condoned by God; (2) some of the violence in the Old Testament was a protection against hostile powers and the judgment of God; (3) the nation of Israel in the Old Testament was a theocracy; and (4) it is obvious from reading the New Testament that from that point on, an entirely different set of ethics applies with the coming kingdom of God with Jesus.[7]

Dietrich also points out, "The Hebrew Scriptures are not a primer on violence, but, in a surprising fullness and diversity, offer guidance for overcoming violence."[8] He shows how biblical passages guide the readers to hinder, limit, reject, and prevent violence, and to eliminate its causes, all the while offering hope of an ultimate end to violence.[9] Brueggemann argues "Yahweh

3. Feinberg, "Peace," 896.
4. Roehrs, *Concordia Self-Study Commentary*, 18.
5. Roehrs, 18.
6. Roehrs, 18.
7. Copan, *Is God a Moral Monster?*, 20–22.
8. Dietrich, "Mark of Cain," 6.
9. Dietrich, 3–11.

is said to work violence that belongs to the enforcement of sovereignty."[10] Violence, therefore, is not part of God's creation. Violence is a result of the chaos, alienation, and pride of the fallen humanity (Gen 3:1–14). Violence will not be part of the new kingdom either.[11] Endelbrecht further explains that:

> Genesis 4 begins with a murder and traces how the shadow of violence lengthens until Lamech perverts God's intention for marriage by taking two wives and boasting that he is seventy-seven times more violent than his murderous ancestor Cain (4:23–24). But we also learn of the birth of Seth, through whom God's promise in Genesis 3:15 will continue. God's plan is not stopped by violence. God appoints another seed of the woman to receive the promise and to carry the story forward (Gen 4:25–26).[12]

Engelbrecht concludes, "The promise continues to unfold until it comes at last to the cross. There, Satan tries to derail God's plan by killing the seed of the woman. Once again, God prevails, not by appointing another, but by raising Jesus from the dead in declaration that the work is finished, creation is redeemed."[13]

Confession for God's Deliverance

Psalm 10 is a psalm of lament that moves toward a conclusion in the faithful assertion of God's inevitable goodness and right action on behalf of the victims (Ps 10:17, 18). This vision of ultimate justice is familiar to those who read the Psalms. In the Psalms, the voice of Israel speaks reflecting the nation's historical experience. They protest against injustice and violence and use strong language against Babylon (Ps 137:8, 9).

Alexander notes, "It is the cry of Israel in despair of exile, committing to Yahweh its strongest desire for revenge and trusting Him to do what is right."[14] Psalms such as this one speak to the language of Israel's heart – passionate for God's glory, immersed in the pain, ambiguities, and turmoil of history,

10. Brueggemann, *Theology of the Old Testament*, 381.
11. D. W. Gill, "Violence", 877.
12. Englebrecht, *Lutheran Study Bible*, 11
13. Engelbrecht, 23.
14. Alexander and Rosner, *New Dictionary of Biblical Theology*, 834.

and offering them all to God.[15] By turning to God in distress and addressing him, the petitioner shows his complete dependence on God. To look elsewhere for deliverance would be contrary to God's will. God's presence will inevitably reside with those who are most needy in order to strengthen them from within. God pays attention to the needs of the disadvantaged and the terrorized. God will perform justice for the unfortunate, the abandoned, and all victims. Perhaps an even greater testimony is that which Isaiah and other prophets perceived with regards to the coming end of violence.

Prophecy of a Coming Peaceful Kingdom

These great prophetic testimonies of peace in the Bible appear to be relevant for any who have suffered violence. Isaiah presents a vivid prophetic picture of anticipated peace in which nations "will beat their swords into plowshares and their spears into pruning hooks. Nation will not take up sword against nation, nor will they train for war anymore" (Isa 2:4). This remarkable call reverberates from Isaiah to Micah 4:3 to the foundation of the world and a careful biblical reader cannot also overlook the prophetic passage in Joel 3:9–10. Swords and plowshares are two valuable uses of metal. Each can mutate into the other, allowing people to tend the ground or kill the neighbor. The Old Testament prophets looked forward to a future Savior who would crush violence and become the "Prince of Peace" (Isa 9:6). Waltke comments, "Isaiah outlines this new model of holy war that is a spiritual, not political, kingdom."[16] Laetsch further comments, "This was not a political, but a spiritual kingdom (Hosea 1:7, Zechariah 4:6b; Micah 7:18–20)."[17] Fretheim confronts readers by saying, "If there were no human violence, there would be no divine violence."[18]

This separation between political and spiritual powers comes to its full fruition in the New Testament. The Messiah does not wield a carnal sword that cuts flesh, but a sword that cuts hearts.[19] God turns political and military

15. Alexander and Rosner, 834.

16. Waltke, *Old Testament Theology*, 402.

17. Laetsch, *Minor Prophets*, 267.

18. Fretheim, "I Was Only a Little Angry," 365.

19. Laetsch, 267.

power over to the state, while turning the spiritual power over to Jesus Christ who conquers the real enemy behind the world powers. [20]

New Testament Literature

In order to understand what the New Testament teaches on the subject of violence, the researcher has examined the teaching of Jesus on revenge in Matthew 5:38–42. The researcher has also examined Jesus's teaching on love in Matthew 5:43–48 and Luke 22:35–38.

Jesus's Teaching on Revenge (Matt 5:38–42)

John Stott writes,

> The authority of Jesus is equal to the law, but does not replace it. However, because of His authority as King and Son of God, the Law is reshaped and re-angled, so that instead of emphasizing the difference between Israel and the Gentile nations, the Law is now seen to encourage love for enemies (5:38–48) and a breaking down of the barrier between Jews and Gentiles (15:1–28).[21]

Gibbs gives a clear explanation that "Jesus continues his authoritative exposition of the true divine intent of the Torah. There is a grudging sort of spirit that afflicts mankind by nature – at least, fallen mankind. Do unto others before they do it to you."[22] Given this universal human condition, it was inevitable that some teachers in first-century Judaism would have taken the biblical admonitions regarding just penalties and recompense (Exod 21:24; Lev 24:20; Deut 19:21) and married them. "This [is the] perspective of do what you have to, and be sure to get even."[23] Gibbs concludes, "This is as far away from the Torah's intention as the east is from the west."[24]

Kleinig summarizes how the law's statements about retribution were intended to function, even on the level of legal interactions in non-Israelite societies where "the *lex talionis* was already elaborated quite explicitly (such

20. Laetsch, 267.
21. Stott, *Men with a Message*, 39.
22. Gibbs, *Matthew 1:1–11:1*, 302.
23. Gibbs, 302.
24. Gibbs, 302.

as in Mesopotamia) long before it was mentioned in the Old Testament. It performed two very important functions there in ancient Israel."[25] First, it limited the scope for revenge, which always tended to escalate indiscriminately and endlessly in any tribal society. By it, the principle of equivalence was enshrined in the administration of justice. Second, it treated the life and the body of every person as equal in value regardless of social, racial, and economic status.[26]

In place of a spirit of grudging recompense and quick revenge, Jesus calls his disciples to lives of joyful generosity and real forgiveness. Jesus's teaching is hyperbolic, but it does not mean that he is not serious. Luther says,

> Christ is not telling me to give what I have to any scoundrel that comes along and to deprive my family of it or others who may need it and whom I am obliged to help, and then to suffer want myself and become a burden to others. He is not saying that we should give and lend to everybody, but to him who begs from us, that is, to the one who really needs it.[27]

Gibbs affirms Luther that "His words are to reform our instincts, our quick reactions, and our unwillingness to sacrifice. St. Paul hits very close to this same target with his admonition to not repay evil for evil, but overcome evil with good (Romans 12:18–21)."[28]

Thompson argues that

> this act allows the inferior in the relationship to assert her or his equal humanity with the oppressor, and it forces the oppressor to take stock of the relationship and perhaps of the social system that supports such inequality. It is risky, to be sure, and demands courage, but it is a creative way to challenge an unhealthy relationship and unjust.[29]

If Jesus's disciples will err, let it be on the side of not retaliating, of yielding, of giving, or of being taken advantage of. A backhanded slap on the face is

25. Gibbs, 302.
26. Kleinig, *Leviticus*, 529.
27. Luther, *Luther's Works*, vol. 35, 117.
28. Gibbs, *Matthew 1:1–11:1*, 303.
29. Thompson, *Justice and Peace*, 192.

not assault.[30] Jews in the first century could readily be forced by occupying Roman soldiers to relinquish possessions or even for a time their freedom.[31]

In the strength of eschatological blessings (Matt 5:3–12), Jesus's disciples can learn to exhibit this strong softness, gaining more by giving up what might be theirs by reasonable expectation and by right. Jesus explaining the true meaning of revenge in the law now addresses love for one's neighbor.

Jesus's Teaching on Love (Matt 5:43–48)

The desire to limit one's loving deeds to a particular group manifests itself wherever sinners are. Jesus's teaching in Matthew 5:43–48 rejects a universal tendency, just as he did in Matthew 5:38–42. Scaer writes pointedly,

> The commands to love the enemy and pray for the persecutors are given with the express intent that they must and can be fulfilled in the community of Jesus (5:11). These are not optional. If these commands are not carried out, this community is no longer recognized as belonging to Jesus.[32]

Jesus commands his disciples to love without reference to the worthiness of the person being loved and to pray for others in the same way. Even the enemy and the persecutor must receive the loving deeds and prayers of Jesus's disciples. Gibbs says, "Love in Biblical parlance does not refer to an emotion, but rather to an attitude of good intention that issues forth in appropriate action for the good of the other. It has nothing necessarily to do with liking someone or with emotions."[33]

His disciples' purpose in loving and praying in this way is to give the evidence that they are the sons of the heavenly Father, who is known only in Jesus (Matt 11:27). The Father is good to both evil and good, to just and unjust. This is so in the realm of creation, where God does not withhold his good gifts from those who have set themselves against him in unbelief and rebellion

30. Jeffrey A. Gibbs clarifies that commentators may be correct in supposing that a slap specifically on the right cheek (5:19) is likely a backhand slap, since most people are right-handed.

31. Keener, *IVP Bible Background Commentary*, 199, writes that Roman soldiers "could requisition what they required and legally demand local inhabitants to provide forced labor (Matthew 27:32)."

32. Scaer, *Sermon on the Mount*, 137–38.

33. Gibbs, *Matthew 1:1–11:1*, 306.

(Rom 3:23, 6:23). It is preeminently so in Jesus himself, who gave his life as the ransom for all (Matt 20:28). In this literary and canonical context, Jesus's primary aim is not to condemn his disciples as the sinners that they surely are, but rather to reveal to his disciples the will of God for their calling as the salt of the earth and light of the world (Matt 5:13–16). Their relationship with Jesus and with his Father is created by repentance (Matt 4:17) and faith in the promised blessings that Jesus pronounced in the Beatitudes (Matt 5:3–12). In that relationship and strengthened by that blessing, Jesus's disciples will individually, and corporately, begin to manifest the will of God for their lives. They know all the while that their quest for perfection has nothing to do with causing or maintaining their standing in the presence of God. Jesus the Lord is the one who manifests absolute perfection on behalf of his disciples, and his completed work for them is at all times the certain hope and confidence of his disciples (Matt 5:19).

Buy a Sword (Luke 22:35–38)

Jesus's final words to the disciples seem to reverse the instructions he gave in Luke 9:1–6 and 10:1–12 when he sent the Twelve and the seventy-two respectively to preach the kingdom of God and to heal. Just writes, "Then He sent them without provisions so they would have to depend on God to sustain them through the gifts offered by their host families, much as a pastor is supported by his congregation (cf 10:6)."[34]

Is Jesus changing his mind? Is he instituting a new pattern for mission? Why does Jesus not instruct his disciples to provide for themselves and even arm themselves for violent conflict by selling their garment and buying a sword? In Acts, the disciples hold everything in common, renouncing their individual possessions (Acts 2–4). They willingly endure persecution and offer no armed resistance (Acts 5, 7, 8, 12, 16, 17, and 19). Hengel believes the Jesus's teaching of nonviolence demanded of his followers that they renounce violence and love their enemies.[35] It may be inferred that Jesus had taken no exception to them bearing the ordinary means of self-defense when traveling

34. Just, *Luke 9:51–24:53*, 851.

35. Hengel, *Victory Over Violence*, 88.

in bandit-infested country beyond the protection of armed authority.[36] Keener comments,

> Protecting Jesus was a paramount issue, yet Jesus did not want His disciples to protect him (cf. 5:44). For Matthew, Jesus came to conquer by way of suffering on the cross, not by way of wielding the sword. Yet it is easier, in human terms, for disciples to fight for their cause than simply to embrace martyrdom for it without resistance; once they realized that martyrdom without resistance was the price for following Jesus, the disciples fled.[37]

Jesus had already plainly affirmed that in the process of fulfilling his mission, he would die a violent death. It was not appropriate for the disciples to attempt to prevent this.

Keener further comments, "They came prepared for armed resistance from one they suppose is a messianic revolutionary. These are not the words of a violent revolutionary (26:47)."[38] Keener believes that the "end-time schemes often included a great battle between the people of the light and the people of darkness, and Jesus certainly expected violence (24:1–2), but His own followers were to stay clear of it."[39] It is to be observed that Jesus only commanded Peter to put his sword back in its place but he did not tell him to throw it away, destroy it, or not to use it again in any situations. In this circumstance, it was wrong to fight, but Jesus was not prohibiting the use of the sword in self-defense, as it is made clear in his command of Luke 22. Jesus's words seem to apply to mission. While Jesus was with the disciples during his earthly ministry they were protected from deprivation of life's necessities (Luke 9:10–17). Just writes, "The period of physical safety is drawing to a close. When Jesus is arrested, the lives of the disciples will be in jeopardy too."[40]

In subsequent church history, the disciples must plan carefully and take precautions if they are to complete their work as God intends (Matt 26:47–54). They will face spiritual enemies and physical need, assault, and martyrdom. They must equip themselves in all respects for the battle ahead. When Paul

36. Hengel, 23.
37. Keener, *Gospel of Matthew*, 642.
38. Keener, *IVP Bible Background Commentary*, 208.
39. Keener, 122.
40. Just, *Luke 9:51–24:53*, 851.

urges Christians to arm themselves with the full armor of God (Eph 6:10–20), he recognizes that true enemies are spiritual, and so the essential weaponry is as well. Just writes, "Yet even though the kingdom of God does not come by the sword, physical provisions for the labor of ministry and the bodily necessities of those who serve will be required."[41]

Jesus is speaking with great irony. The disciples have exhibited a pattern of misunderstanding throughout their sojourn with him. They still do not comprehend that, in the kingdom, the things of God are opposite to the things of people.[42] In this respect, they are sinners who think about their own needs and do not trust the Lord of the harvest to provide. They have been sent as messengers of peace, but like Jerusalem (Luke 19:42), they do not yet truly understand the things that make for peace, as shown by the two swords they have in their possession at Passover. They are among the transgressors whom Jesus came to save.[43]

Just writes, "The two swords suggest the apostles were afraid and so brought swords to defend themselves by violence. Hence, the apostles are among the transgressors. But this citation primarily sets the stage for the passion that is to follow. From this moment on, Jesus will be reckoned with transgressors."[44] These precise words conform to Luke's view of Jesus as the suffering, righteous prophet who comes to identify with sinful humanity, place himself in solidarity with sinners, and die on behalf of all, crucified between two malefactors.[45]

His Kingdom Is Not of This World (John 18:36)

At his trial, Jesus answered, "My kingdom is not of this world. If my kingdom were of this world, my servants would have been fighting, that I might not be delivered over to the Jews. But my kingdom is not from this world" (John 18:36 ESV). Jesus's clear statement shows that God's kingdom is not defended by force of counter violence. Rather, he is pointing out specifically that his was a spiritual kingdom. This spiritual kingdom has enough resources of its own

41. Just, 852.
42. Just, 852.
43. Just, 852.
44. Just, 853.
45. Just, 853.

to be victorious if it were to be engaged in an actual physical violence with the kingdom of the world (Matt 26:53). Jesus was rejecting any worldly political aspirations or rebellious intent. His kingdom did not threaten the external rule of the Roman Empire (Luke 20:25). Engelbrecht believes that "legitimate public ordinances are good creations of God and divine ordinances, which a Christian can safely use."[46]

Do Not Murder (Matt 5:21–23)

One of the most revolutionary teachings of Jesus is that human violence starts in a deeper place. The mind of violence has already begun before blood is spilled or words wound. In the Sermon on the Mount, Jesus said, "You have heard that it was said to the people long ago, 'you shall not murder, and anyone who murders will be subject to judgment.' But I tell you that anyone who is angry with his brother or sister will be subject to judgment" (Matt 5:21–23). We cannot talk about murder without talking about rage. We cannot talk about burning of churches, bombings, and taking of lives in Northern Nigeria without talking about the infections of hatred, malice, and anger in a violent culture. Again, there is this important teaching from Mark 7:14–15: "Again Jesus called the crowd to him and said, 'Listen to me, everyone, and understand this. Nothing outside a person can defile them by going into them. Rather, it is what comes out of a person that defiles them.'"

Here is the crux of the matter and it is the ugly news of the human condition that violence, like all sins, comes out of the human heart. Violence appears not to be caused by what people see in movies. External stimuli certainly affect people. Deep psychological wounding also conditions people. A culture of violence tends to give permission to be violent, and to be desensitized, but the instinct and choice to act out in violence comes out of the heart. I am not saying that this statement of Jesus offers a complete psychology for violence. But there is a kernel of truth here that may serve us well as we look at the mystery of violence in our society, especially in context of Christians in Northern Nigeria. The Pharisees wanted to believe that sin was a matter of what people put in, like food they ate. That is the convenient way to look at life. Far more troubling, but true nonetheless, is that all people have within them the potential for violence.

---

46. Engelbrecht, *Lutheran Study Bible*, 1820.

Faithful in the Face of Violence (Matt 10:28)

This aspect leads to a consideration that Jesus encourages us to live bravely in the face of violence. Jesus clearly taught that the world is a sinful and violent place, yet he challenged his followers not to live in fear and trepidation. They are encouraged not to be afraid of those who kill the body but cannot kill the soul. He also encourages his followers that in the world, they will have trouble, but they are to be brave because he has conquered the world (John 16:33). In the context of religious violence in Northern Nigeria, the researcher is concerned that there is the need to ask ourselves the question, what is this bravery of which Jesus speaks? How does this kind of bravery affect church members and others living everyday lives and working in a violent place like Northern Nigeria and other parts of the world where religious violence prevails? How can they take Jesus's teaching to heart so that they do not live their lives cowering?

Response to Violence (Matt 5:9)

Another question is where would Christians in Northern Nigeria turn to in the Scriptures for ways to deal with violence? What does Jesus want congregations to do about violence? The following beatitude comes to mind, which includes this real-life challenge, "Blessed are the peacemakers, for they will be called children of God" (Matt 5:9). What can Christians do about violence? It appears that it must start with a serious commitment to the principle of "blessed are the peacemakers." But it seems that will not happen unless we go beyond wishful thinking. So the question remains, what is this peacemaking?

Peacemaking is active work, hard work, and frustrating work. It is not the convenient thing. Does it not mean blessed are those who expend their lives in the interest of reconciliation and shalom? France comments, "This beatitude goes beyond a merely peaceful disposition to an active attempt to 'make' peace, perhaps by seeking reconciliation with one's enemies, but also more generally by bringing to those who are estranged from one another."[47] Gibbs comments,

> Peacemakers in 5:9 refers to Jesus' disciples as they bring the message of the reign of heaven into the world. The peacemaking

47. France, *Gospel of Matthew*, 169.

> should not be seen as limited only to apostolic or pastoral activity. Blessed are the peacemakers whom God uses to bring the message of the reign of heaven so that others may have the peace that Jesus brings. At the fulfillment of all things, Jesus' peacemaking disciples will be called the "sons of God."[48]

Betz comments, "Peacemaking is a means of involvement in human predicament of war-like conditions. Coping with such conditions corresponds to God's own response and action. It implies assuming responsibility against all the odds, risking peacemaking out of the situation of powerlessness, and demonstrating the conviction that in the end God's kingdom will prevail."[49]

The challenge is not palatable. But it is Jesus's clear call for his followers in all times. Somehow, the message and work of peacemakers needed to have begun long before the bullets are loaded for violence in contemporary Northern Nigeria. Bonhoeffer wrote, "The followers of Jesus have been called to peace. When He called them they found their peace, for He is their peace. They are told that they must not only have peace but make it. And to that end, they renounce all violence and tumult."[50]

Stott says, "Now peacemaking is a divine work. For peace means reconciliation and God is the author of peace and of reconciliation. Peacemakers who sow in peace raise a harvest of righteousness."[51] Carson is of the belief that when responding to violence, "one's manifestation of love for enemies will be in prayer; praying for an enemy and loving him will prove mutually reinforcing and he sums it up saying, the more love, the more prayer, the more prayer, the more love."[52] Another question to ask is, how about evoking counter violence? In the Old Testament, the researcher examined how personal rights are protected by a divinely established system of retribution. Since the community of believers is not a national nation as Israel, there is no room in Jesus's model for retaliation. Bonhoeffer reiterates: "The only way to overcome evil is to let it run itself to a standstill because it does not find the resistance it is looking for. Violence stands condemned by its failure to evoke

48. Gibbs, *Matthew 1:1–11:1*, 253.

49. Betz, *Sermon on the Mount*, 140.

50. Bonhoeffer, *Cost of Discipleship*, 102.

51. Stott, *Message of the Sermon on the Mount*, 50–51.

52. Carson, *"Matthew"*, 158.

counter-violence."[53] However, Anderson agrees with Jesus's teaching in part, saying, "In regard to violence or the use of force, Jesus forbade His disciples to indulge in personal retaliation of any sort."[54] But he does not believe that this means that a "Christian should stand idly by while a baby is kicked to death or a woman is raped, for example."[55] Stumme rightly observes that our Christian witness "takes on a critical edge when we trust our moral activity to achieve what comes only as God's gift of faith."[56] This biblical and theological imperative may remind us Christians in Northern Nigeria that our relationship with God is not something we can earn through our own energy, but it is God's gift to which we respond in faith. The heart of Christians' response to violence is to clarify, reinforce, restore, and promote an understanding of God's gracious gift in bearing the witness to Jesus Christ.

Briscoe assures Christians that "the reality of conflict in human relations is that evil will continue to persist and Christians will not be exempt from its painful encroachment."[57] So far, our study in the New Testament shows that with the teaching and example of Jesus Christ, God's clear will for Christians in a violent world is that they stand firm in their faith. We are further encouraged with the words of Gill that the New Testament response of peacemaking, patient suffering, non-retaliation even for an unjust cause, and overcoming evil with good, dominates the text.[58] Collier reiterates, "For Christians, non-violence is rooted in our understanding of a God who is peace, who gives peace, who calls us to make peace and justice, and to live out Jesus's teachings and bear witness to the promise of God."[59] Vicedom believes "the suffering of the church has greater witnessing power than the Word alone."[60]

The secondary motifs in the New Testament remind Christians that some people of God may find themselves in military or police posts (Acts 10). And God intends to use those who bear the sword to punish evil and protect the

53. Bonhoeffer, *Cost of Discipleship*, 127.

54. Anderson, *Teaching of Jesus*, 143.

55. Anderson, 143.

56. Stumme and Bloomquist, "Introduction," 1.

57. Briscoe, *Communicator's Commentary: Romans*, 228.

58. Gill, "Violence" 878

59. Collier, *Living Faithfully in a Violent World: Walking with Jesus' Path of Peace* (Minneapolis: Augsburg Fortress, 2001), 11.

60. Vicedom, *Mission of God*, 138.

good (Rom 13:3–5). This spiritual warfare is carried out by means of faith, prayer, and the gospel. Violence is replaced by creative, nonviolent alternatives. It is absorbed with patient suffering and forgiving love.[61] This is already realized in God's established kingdom through Jesus Christ (Luke 17:21b; Heb 9:15, 12:24).

The New Testament literature reveals that Jesus gives gifts to the church for spiritual power and not for militant response to violence (Eph 4:7–13). The Christians' battleground is in the spiritual realm against the forces of Satan and spiritual warfare by putting on the full power of God's own spiritual armor (Eph 6:12–13).[62] Jesus never defined the mission of the New Testament church by conquest of land and or people. Its mission is to encourage the free submission of souls to the will of God and to recognize the dignity of all human beings as bearers of God's image, in which all carnal weapons are renounced (Matt 26:50–56; 2 Cor 10:4, 5). The New Testament teaching clearly shows that a violent end awaits Satan and his cohorts at the end of human history (Rev 19:11–15; 20:1–10). Schulz concludes, "The church must learn to listen in order to respond to cries and the crises of our time."[63]

Martin Luther's Works

The Luther section is important to the issues of Christian response to violence because it deals with the subject of civil obedience or disobedience that is central in the history of Lutheranism. This will enhance Christian understanding of the subject of violence to world Christianity.

The Augsburg Confession declares that human beings cannot be justified before God by their powers, merits, or works, but they are justified as a gift on account of Christ through faith when they believe that they are received into grace and that their sins are forgiven on account of Christ, who by his death made sanctification for our sins.[64] Martin Luther understood Christians in particular as "Saint and Sinner."[65] In his exposition of Deuteronomy 6:1–5,

61. Vicedom, 877.
62. Kunhiyop, *African Christian Ethics*, 115.
63. Schulz, *Mission from the Cross*, 301.
64. The Augsburg Confession IV in, Kolb and Wengert, *Book of Concord*, 38–41.
65. Luther, *Luther's Works*, vol. 9, 65–69.

Luther maintains that while God may work through particular people and institutions, establishing peace is a work that God alone can perform. "It is not the work of a prince or any government."[66] Here Luther does not mean that we should not work for peace, but that true and authentic peace is God's gift and work. The good news that Christians share is in the person of Jesus and the love of God is for and with them in all that they face. As children of God, it is required that they confess that the way they live, and the way they respond to violence is their response to God's love for them in Christ Jesus and not something they do in order to earn God's favor. It is best to let Luther speak through his works himself.[67] Luther's ethical idea could be understood from his statements including *On God, the Creator, The Believer, and Law; Law and Gospel; Faith and Works of Love to the Neighbor*; *The Worldly Regiment and Political Use of the Law*; and *The Civil Realm and Christian Duty*. There is the need to examine these statements sequentially.

God, the Creator, the Believer, and Law

Luther says, "I hold and believe that I am God's creature, that is, that he has given me and constantly sustains my body, soul, and life, my members great and small, all my senses, my reason and understanding, and the like . . ."[68] and "All this he does out of pure love and goodness, without our merit, as a kind of father who cares for us so that no evil may befall us."[69] God is "an eternal fountain that overflows with pure goodness from whom pours forth all that is truly good."[70] Concerning our ethical obligations, Luther says, "For all this it is my duty to thank and praise, serve and obey him."[71] According to Luther, ethics means a relationship with norms and for Christians that relationship is personal. God is the norm. For Luther, there are two kinds of laws – human law and law of God. Luther offers the following explanation to differentiate them when he says,

66. Luther, 65–69.
67. Luther, 65–69.
68. Kolb and Wengert, *Book of Concord*, 49.
69. Kolb and Wengert, 389, 432–33.
70. Kolb and Wengert, 389.
71. Luther, *Luther's Works*, vol. 35, 366.

> the little word "law" you must here not take in human fashion as a teaching about what works are to be done or not done. That is the way with human laws: a law fulfilled by works, even though there is no heart in the doing of them. But God judges according to what is in the depths of the heart. Hence all men are called liars . . . for everyone finds in himself displeasure in what is good and pleasure what is bad. If now, there is no willing pleasure in the good, then the inmost heart is not set on the law of God. Then, too, there is surely sin, and God's wrath is deserved, even though outwardly there seem to be many good deeds and honorable life.[72]

Law and Gospel

In discussing the law of Moses, the natural law, and the gospel in the New Testament, Luther affirms, "Thus, I keep the commandments which Moses has given, not because Moses gave the commandment, but because they are implanted in me by nature and Moses agrees exactly with nature."[73] "We will regard Moses as a teacher, but we will not regard him as a lawgiver – unless he agrees with both the New Testament and the natural law."[74] In answer to the question, Why does one then keep and teach the Ten Commandments?, Luther says, "Because the natural laws were never so orderly and well written as by Moses. Therefore it is reasonable to follow the example of Moses."[75]

> Thus, "Thou shalt not kill, commit adultery, steal, etc." are not Mosaic laws only, but also natural law written in each man's heart, as St. Paul teaches (Romans 2[:15]). Also Christ Himself (Matthew 7 [:12]) includes all the law and the prophets in this natural law, "So whatever you wish that men would do to you, do so to them; for this is the law and the prophets." Paul does the same thing in Romans 13[:9], where he sums up all the commandments of Moses in the love which also the natural law teaches in the words, "Love your neighbor as yourself." . . .

72. Luther, 366.
73. Luther, 168.
74. Luther, 165.
75. Luther, *Luther's Works*, vol. 40, 98.

> Otherwise, were it not naturally written in the heart, one would have to teach and preach the law for a long time before it became the concern of conscience. The heart must also find and feel the law in itself. Otherwise, it would become a matter of conscience for no one. However, the devil so blinds and possesses hearts, that they do not always feel this law. Therefore one must preach the law and impress it on the minds of people till God assists and enlightens them, so that they feel in their hearts what the Word says.[76]

Therefore,

> Moses' legislation about images and the Sabbath, and what else goes beyond the natural law, is free, null and void, and is specifically given to the Jewish people alone. It is as when an emperor or a king makes special laws and ordinances in his territory, as the Sachsenspiegel in Saxony. . . . Therefore, one is to let Moses be the Sachsenspiegel of the Jews and not confuse us gentiles with it, just as the Sachsenspiegel is not observed in France, though the natural law there is in agreement with it.[77]

What use then, is the law? "The law commands and requires us to do certain things."[78]

> Key to God's law is man's motivation; to fulfill the law, however, is to do its works with pleasure and love, to live a godly and good life of one's own accord, without the compulsion of the law. This pleasure and love for the law is put into the heart by the Holy Spirit. But the Holy Spirit is not given except in, with, and by faith in Jesus Christ, as St. Paul says in the introduction. Faith, moreover, comes only through God's Word or Gospel, which preaches Christ, saying that he is God's Son and a man.[79]

"A good and just decision must not and cannot be pronounced out of books, but must come from a free mind, as though there were no books. Such a free

76. Luther, 97.
77. Luther, 97.
78. Luther, *Luther's Works*, vol. 35, 162.
79. Luther, 368.

decision is given, however, by love and by natural law, with which all reason is filled; out of the books come extravagant and untenable judgments."[80]

Luther provides the following story of Duke Charles of Burgundy:

> A certain nobleman took an enemy prisoner. The prisoner's wife came to ransom her husband. The nobleman promised to give back the husband on condition that she would lie with him. The woman was virtuous, yet wished to set her husband free; so she goes and asks her husband whether she should do this thing in order to set him free. The husband wished to be set free and to save his life, so he gives his wife permission. After the nobleman had lain with the wife, he had the husband beheaded the next day and gave him to her as a corpse. She laid the whole case before Duke Charles. He summoned the nobleman and commanded him to marry the woman. When the wedding day was over he had the nobleman beheaded, gave the woman possession of his property, and restored her to honor. Thus he punished the crime in a princely way.[81]

"Now, it has to be observed that no pope, no jurist, no law book could have given him such a decision. It sprang from untrammeled reason, above the law in all the books, and is so excellent that everyone must approve of it and find the justice of it written in his own heart."[82]

On Faith and Works of Love to the Neighbor

Luther, in the preface to *St. Paul's Epistle to the Romans*, notes that faith is "a living, busy, active, mighty thing, this faith. It is impossible for it not to be doing good works incessantly. It does not ask whether good works are to be done, but before the question is asked, it has already done them, and is constantly doing them."[83] Faith, however, is "a divine work in us which changes us and makes us to be born anew of God, John 1[:12–13]. It kills the Old Adam and makes us altogether different men, in heart and spirit and mind and

80. The example is from Luther, *Luther's Works*, vol. 45, 128, in which it says good rulers rule not according to books, but according to love and natural law.

81. Luther, *Luther's Works*, vol. 45, 128.

82. Luther, 128.

83. Luther, *Luther's Works*, vol. 35, 370.

powers; and it brings with it the Holy Spirit."[84] "For through faith a man becomes free from sin and comes to take pleasure in God's commandments."[85] About the freedom of the Christian, Luther says, "A Christian is a perfectly free lord of all, subject to none. A Christian is perfectly dutiful servant of all, subject to all."[86] He further argues, "Man has a twofold nature, a spiritual and a bodily one. According to the spiritual nature, which men refer to as the soul, he is called a spiritual inner or new man. According to the bodily nature, which men refer to as flesh, he is called a carnal, outward, or old man. Because of this diversity of nature the Scriptures assert contradictory things concerning the same man, since these two men in the same man contradict each other."[87]

According to Luther,

> The nature of this priesthood and kingship is illustrated: First, with respect to the kingship, every Christian is by faith so exalted above all things that, by virtue of a spiritual power, he is lord of all things without exception, so that nothing can do him any harm. . . . This is not to say that every Christian is placed over all things to have and control them by physical power . . . for such power belongs to kings, princes, and other men on earth. Our ordinary experience in life shows us that we are subjected to all, suffer many things, and even die.[88]

Luther says, "A man does not live for himself alone in this mortal body to work for it alone, but he lives also for all men on earth; rather he lives only for others and not for himself."[89]

Luther maintains that "his is a truly Christian life. Here faith is truly active through love [Galatians 5:6], that is, it finds expression in works of the freest service, cheerfully and lovingly done, with which a man willingly serves another without hope of reward; and for himself he is satisfied with the fullness

84. Luther, 370.

85. Luther, 371.

86. Luther, *Luther's Works*, vol. 31, 344.

87. Luther, 344.

88. Luther, 354.

89. Luther, 364.

and wealth of his faith."[90] Concerning showing love for the neighbor, Luther makes the following explanation:

> Behold, from faith thus flow forth love and joy in the Lord, and from love a joyful, willing, and free mind that serves one's neighbor willingly and takes no account of gratitude and ingratitude, of praise or blame, of gain or loss. For a man does not serve, that he may put men under obligations. He does not distinguish between friends and enemies or anticipate their thankfulness or not thankful, but he most freely and most willingly spends himself and all that he has, whether he wastes all on the thankless or whether he gains a reward.[91]

Therefore, according to Luther, "As our heavenly Father has in Christ freely come to our aid, we also ought freely to help our neighbor through our body and its works and each one should become as it were a Christ to the other that we may be Christ's to one another and Christ may be the same in all, that is, that we may be truly Christians."[92]

Conclusion

Luther closes by saying, "We conclude, therefore, that a Christian lives not in himself, but in Christ and in his neighbor. Otherwise he is not a Christian. He lives in Christ through faith, in his neighbor through love. By faith he is caught up beyond himself into God. By love he descends beneath himself into his neighbor. Yet he always remains in God and in his love."[93] Luther proceeds with the discussion on the ethical obligation of Christians explained from his two kinds of righteousness.[94] Luther says there are two kinds of Christian righteousness.

> The first is the alien righteousness that is the righteousness of another, instilled from without. This is the righteousness of Christ by which he justifies through faith. Therefore everything which

90. Luther, 365.
91. Luther, 367.
92. Luther, 367–68.
93. Luther, 371.
94. Luther, 297–300.

> Christ has is ours graciously bestowed on us unworthy men out of God's sheer mercy. Through faith in Christ, therefore Christ's righteousness becomes our righteousness and all that he has becomes ours; rather He Himself becomes ours. This righteousness is primary; it is the basis, the cause, the source of all our own actual righteousness. For this is the righteousness given in place of the original righteousness lost in Adam. It accomplishes the same as that original righteousness would have accomplished; rather, it accomplishes more. Therefore this is alien righteousness.[95]

The second kind of righteousness is "our proper righteousness, not because we alone work it, but because we work with that first and alien righteousness. In the second place, this righteousness consists in love to one's neighbor."[96] "This righteousness is the product of the righteousness of the first type, actually its fruit and consequence. . . .This righteousness goes on to complete the first for it ever strives to do away with the old Adam and to destroy the body of sin. Therefore it hates itself and loves its neighbor; it does not seek its own good, but that of another, and in this way its whole way of living consists. For in that it hates itself and does not seek its own, it crucifies the flesh."[97]

> Because it seeks the good of another, it works love. Thus in each sphere it does God's will, living soberly with self, justly with neighbor, devoutly toward God. This is what Paul also says, "Let this mind be in you, which was also in Christ Jesus" (Philippians 2:5). This means you should be as inclined and disposed toward one another as you see Christ was disposed toward you. How? Thus, surely, that "though he was in the form of a God, [he] did not count equality with God a thing to be grasped, but emptied himself, taking the form of a servant" (Philippians 2:6–7). The Apostle means that each individual shall become the servant of another in accordance with the example of Christ. It is in this way, then, that one takes on the form of a servant. Through love

95. Luther, 297–99.

96. Luther, 299–305.

97. Luther, 299–305.

> we are servants of one another. And if we do not freely desire to put off that form of God and take on the form of a servant, let us be compelled to do so against our will. It ought to wish that its neighbor's condition were better that its own, and if its neighbor's condition is the better, it ought to rejoice no less than it rejoices when its own is the better.[98]

Luther says, "This pertains to private individuals who do not desire vengeance. On the other hand, in accordance with the Gospel (Matthew 5:40) to those who would take their coats, they are prepared to give their cloaks as well, and they do not resist any evil. These are the sons of God, brothers of Christ, heirs of future blessings."[99]

The Worldly Regiment and the Political Use of the Law

Luther maintains that the worldly regiment belongs to the kingdom of God, and the political use of the law to the kingdom of the world. Those who belong to the kingdom of God are all true believers who are in Christ and under Christ.[100]

> These people need no temporal law or sword. If all the world were composed of real Christians, that is, true believers, there would be no need for or benefits from prince, king, lord, sword, or law. They would serve no purpose, since Christians have in their heart the Holy Spirit, who both teaches and makes them to do injustice to no one, to love everyone, and to suffer injustice and even death willingly and cheerfully at the hands of anyone. For this reason it is impossible that the temporal sword and law should find any work to do among Christians, since they do of their own accord much more than any laws and teachings can demand.[101]

---

98. Luther, 299–305.
99. Luther, 299–305.
100. Luther, *Luther's Works*, vol. 45, 88–89.
101. Luther, 88–89.

"The law has been laid down for the lawless . . . so that those who are not Christians may through the law be restrained outwardly from evil deeds."[102]

If the world were to be left to sinners without their restraint, "the world would be reduced to chaos. For this reason God has ordained two governments regiments: regiment implies that God has a rule over creation: the spiritual, by which the Holy Spirit produces Christians and righteous people under Christ; and the temporal, which restrains the un-Christian and wicked so that they are obliged to keep still and maintain an outward peace."[103] Luther says, "For this reason one must carefully distinguish between these two governments. Both must be permitted to remain; the one to produce righteousness, the other to bring about external peace and prevent evil deeds."[104] Luther maintains,

> Here the other proposition applies, that you are under obligation to serve and assist the sword by whatever means you can. . . . For it is something which you do not need, but which is very beneficial and essential for the whole world and for your neighbor. Therefore, if you see that there is a lack of hangmen, constables, judges, lords, or princes, and you find that you are qualified, you should offer your services and seek the position that the essential governmental authority may not be despised and become enfeebled or perish.[105]

Luther says it is done only "for the good of your neighbor and for the maintenance of the safety and peace of others,"[106] and in doing this "you must not consider your personal interests and how you may remain lord, but those of your subjects to whom you owe help and protection, that such action may proceed in love."[107]

102. Luther, 90.
103. Luther, 91.
104. Luther, 92.
105. Luther, 95.
106. Luther, 96.
107. Luther, 125.

The Civil Realm and Christian Duty

In "Whether Soldiers, Too, Can Be Saved," Luther affirms the legitimacy of the military profession.[108] He identifies it with the divine institution of the sword to punish evil, protect the good, and preserve peace. Luther candidly admits that the military calling can be abused, but misuse by no means invalidates its legitimacy and function.[109] In developing this basic thesis, Luther discusses how a soldier must execute his God-given office. First, Luther deals with the question of fighting against overlords, that is, the legitimate government. To do this is to rebel against the order instituted by God.[110] The Reformer is quite aware that there are rulers who distort, abuse, and debase their office; nonetheless, their misconduct cannot harm men's souls.[111] Second, Luther treats the question of if a soldier may fight in a war in which equals war against equals. Here he articulates the principle of self-defense. A ruler is charged by God to defend and protect his people when they have been attacked, and to do this he needs soldiers who serve him because God has appointed him to be ruler.[112]

Luther, however, cautions that a soldier must not trust in the justness of the cause for which he fights. Confidence and trust must be in God, who alone gives victory. Finally, the question of whether soldiers may participate in wars waged by rulers against their subjects is treated under each of the following headings.

Soldiery is Permitted

In "Whether Soldiers, Too, Can Be Saved,"[113] Luther takes the position that "soldiery is a legitimate vocation which belongs to the God-given office of the sword. In this book Luther endorses and expounds the principle of defense as the divinely appointed duty of every government."[114] Luther clearly endorses the office of the soldier. "In the first place, we must distinguish between an occupation and the man who holds it, between a work and the man who does

108. Luther, *Luther's Works*, vol. 46, 90–137.

109. Luther, 90–137.

110. Luther, 90–137.

111. Luther, 90–137.

112. Luther, 246.

113. Luther, 87.

114. Luther, 247.

it. An occupation or a work can be good and right in it and yet be bad and wrong if the man who does the work is evil or wrong or does not do his work properly."[115] This is the case even though soldiery seems to do terrible things in the world. "In the same way, when I think of a soldier fulfilling his office by punishing the wicked, killing the wicked, and creating so much misery, it seems an un-Christian work completely contrary to Christian love. But when I think of how it protects the good and keeps and preserves wife and child, house and farm, property, and honor and peace, then I see how precious and godly this work is."[116] Luther rejects the objection that Christians have not been commanded to fight according to Matthew 5:39–42. He states,

> Indeed Christians do not fight and have no worldly rulers among them. Their government is a spiritual government, and according to the Spirit, they are subjects of no one but Christ. Nevertheless, as far as body and property are concerned, they are subject to worldly rulers and owe them obedience. If worldly rulers call upon them to fight, then they ought to and must fight and be obedient, not as Christians, but as members of the state and obedient subjects. Christians therefore do not fight as individuals or for their own benefit, but as obedient servants of the authorities under whom they live. This is what St. Paul wrote to Titus when he said that Christians should obey the authorities [Titus 3:1]. The office of the soldier belongs to the office of the sword.[117]

Luther summarizes,

> The office of the sword is in itself right and is a divine and useful ordinance, which God does not want us to despise, but to fear, honor, and obey, under penalty of punishment, as St. Paul says in Romans 13[:1–5]. For God has established two kinds of government among men. The one is spiritual; it has no sword, but it has the word, by means of which men are to become good and righteous, so that with this righteousness they may attain eternal

115. Luther, 94.

116. Luther, 96.

117. Luther, 247.

> life. He administers this righteousness through the Word, which he has committed to the preachers. The other kind is worldly government, which works through the sword so that those who do not want to be good and righteous to eternal life may be forced to become good and righteous in the eyes of the world. He administers this righteousness through the sword. And although God will not reward this kind of righteousness with eternal life, nonetheless, he still wishes peace to be maintained among men and rewards them with the temporal blessings.[118]

Luther maintains that "God himself is the founder, lord, master, protector, and rewarder of both kinds of righteousness."[119] However, as with all offices, the incumbents of such offices could abuse their office. But it is difficult to apply hard and fast laws how they should act. "And here we have to face the fact that it is impossible to establish hard and fast rules and laws in this matter. There are so many cases and so many exceptions to any rule that it is very difficult or even impossible to decide everything accurately and equitably. If we do not make exceptions and strictly follow the law we do the greatest injustice of all."[120] People do things not always with the same kind of motives (for example, the kiss of Judas versus the kiss of the rest of the disciples).[121]

War and Resistance against a Tyrant

There are three kinds of people fighting war: (1) an equal against an equal, (2) an overlord may fight against his subjects, and (3) a subject may fight against his overlord. Luther now addresses the third group and raises the question of rebellion and the ousting of a tyrant from his office. The question is to what degree may that be allowed and legitimate? "Therefore the question here is whether a situation can ever develop in which it is just for people to act against this law, to be disobedient to rulers and fight against them, depose them, or put them in bonds."[122] Luther acknowledges the fact that history has shown that the Greeks, the Romans, and the Jews (1 Kgs 15:25–29) deposed,

118. Luther, 100.
119. Luther, 100.
120. Luther, 100.
121. Luther, 101–2.
122. Luther, 103.

killed, and expelled worthless and wicked rulers.[123] But Luther rejects such action, saying, "I have never known a case in which this was a just action, and even now I cannot imagine any."[124] Just because the lord or king is unjust does not mean that his subjects should be unjust in return. "On the contrary, we ought to suffer wrong, and if a prince or lord will not tolerate the gospel we ought to go into another realm according to Matthew 10:[23]." In terms of an insane ruler it would be correct to depose him, "for he would not be considered a man since his reason is gone."[125] A tyrant however is different because "he still knows that he is doing wrong. He still has a conscience and his faculties. There is also hope that he may improve and permit someone to talk to him and instruct him and follow this advice."[126] Killing a tyrant has many downsides. In deposing a tyrant, "the practice spreads and it becomes a commonplace thing arbitrarily to call men tyrants who are not tyrants, and even to kill them if the mob takes a notion to do so."[127] "If injustice is to be suffered, then it is better for subjects to suffer it from their rulers than for the rulers to suffer it from their subjects."[128]

The outcome of ousting a tyrant has always been tragic. Examples from Denmark and ancient civilized empires show this. God says, "Vengeance is mine, I will repay" (Rom 12:9) and "Judge not" (Matt 7:1). "No one can deny that when subjects set themselves against their rulers. They avenge themselves and make themselves judges."[129] The authority of justice and revenge belongs to God. "What would become of the world if everyone who was in the right punished everyone who did wrong? The servant would strike his master, the maid her mistress, the children the parents, the pupils the teacher. That would be a fine state of affairs."[130] This applies also to the objection that one cannot live under all that cruelty imposed and endure it no longer because of the wicked tyrant. But Luther remains firm even then, saying, "To these I

123. Luther, 104.
124. Luther, 104.
125. Luther, 105.
126. Luther, 105.
127. Luther, 105.
128. Luther, 106, 113–14.
129. Luther, 107.
130. Luther, 114.

say that rulers are not to be opposed with violence and rebellion."[131] Luther's reluctance to endorse resistance is partly based on his negative experience of the peasant revolts. They had been bloody, mob-like uprisings. "Therefore, the preservation of the rulers whom God has appointed is a matter that rests with God and in his hands alone."[132] "Therefore I advise everyone who wants to act with a good conscience in this matter to be satisfied with the worldly rulers and not attack them."[133] We should also remain realistic of our own existence in this imperfect world. The ideal will never exist. "God has thrown us into the world, under the power of the devil. As a result we have no paradise here. Rather, at any time we can expect all kinds of misfortune to body, wife, child, property, and honor."[134] In summary to this point, "That is enough that war and uprisings against our superiors cannot be right."[135]

Just War

What about war between two equals? "At the very outset I want to say that whoever starts a war is in the wrong."[136] The war is a matter of self-defense. "Self-defense is a proper ground for fighting and therefore all laws agree that self-defense shall go unpunished; and he who kills another in self-defense is innocent in the eyes of all men."[137]

> Let this be, then, the first thing to be said in this matter. No war is just, even if it is a war between equals, unless one has such a good reason for fighting and such a good conscience that he can say, "My neighbor compels and forces me to fight, though I would rather avoid it." In that case, it can be called not only war, but lawful self-defense, for we must distinguish between wars that someone begins because that is what he wants to do and does before anyone else attacks him, and those wars which are provoked when an attack is made by someone else. The first

131. Luther, 108.
132. Luther, 110.
133. Luther, 112.
134. Luther, 117.
135. Luther, 118.
136. Luther, 118.
137. Luther, 120.

> kind can be called wars of desire; the second, wars of necessity. The first kinds are of the devil; God does not give good fortune to the man who wages that kind of war. The second kinds are human disasters; God help them![138]

The reason for self-defense and just war is simply "that every lord and prince is bound to protect his people and to preserve the peace for them. That is his office; that is why he has the sword (Romans 13[:4])."[139] Even if the war is done in self-defense, there is no reason to relish this opportunity neither to fight back nor to be overconfident. "Even though you are absolutely certain that you are not starting a war but are being forced into one, you shall still fear God and remember him you ought not to think that, that justifies anything you do and plunge headlong into battle."[140]

Conclusion

"War against equals should be waged only when it is forced upon us and then it should be fought in the fear of God. Such a war is forced upon us when an enemy or neighbor attacks and starts the war, and refuses to cooperate in settling the matter according to law or through arbitration and common agreement, or when one overlooks and puts up with the enemy's evil words and tricks, but he still insists on having his own way."[141]

Conscientious Objection and Mercenary Service

The principle Luther establishes is that all soldiers hired to fight must be paid and given food. "Therefore, since it is a legitimate office, ordained by God, they should be paid and compensated for doing it, as Christ says in Matthew 10[:10], 'A laborer deserves his wage.'"[142] A further question is, "Suppose my lords were wrong in going to war; should I obey?" Luther said, "I reply: If you know for sure that he is wrong, then you should fear God rather than men, Acts 4[:29], and you should neither fight nor serve, for you cannot

138. Luther, 121.
139. Luther, 122.
140. Luther, 123.
141. Luther, 125.
142. Luther, 129.

have a good conscience before God."[143] Even if your lord would coerce you to fight and you fear that if you refuse to go to war you would be branded as a coward, Luther answers, "You must take the risk and, with God's help, let whatever happens, happen. He can restore it to you hundredfold, as He promises in the gospel."[144]

Thus, conscientious objection applies also to all other offices. "In every other occupation we are also exposed to the danger that the rulers will compel us to act wrongly; but since God will have us leave even father and mother for his sake, we must certainly leave lords for his sake if they put you to shame or call you disloyal, it is better for God to call you loyal and honorable than for the world to call you loyal and honorable."[145] Mercenary service is wrong. "It follows that those mercenaries who wander about the country seeking war [who] from laziness or roughness and wildness of spirit waste their time, cannot be on good terms with God."[146] Luther continues, "They can neither give God any good explanation for these do not have a good conscience about their wandering. All they have is a foolhardy desire or eagerness for war or to lead the free, wild life which is typical of such people."[147] In the writing *On War Against the Turk*, Luther denied the right of the church to lead any kind of military crusade.[148] The defense of the empire and of its imperiled subjects belonged by divine order solely to the emperor, Luther declared.

Conclusion

Luther concludes that a Christian lives not for himself, but in Christ and for his neighbor. Otherwise, he is not a Christian. Christians therefore do not fight as individuals or for their own benefit, but as obedient servants of the authorities under whom they live.[149] The researcher will now turn to the essential contributing literature to examine the problem of violence in society and how the essential literature responds.

143. Luther, 130.
144. Luther, 130.
145. Luther, 131.
146. Luther, 131.
147. Luther, 134.
148. Luther, 155.
149. Luther, 118.

CHAPTER THREE

Essential Contributing Literature

Early Christian Pacifism

Here we will examine relevant literature relating to the problem of violence during the early church of the first through fourth centuries, and then what current scholars have to say on the problem of violence. The researcher has examined the New Testament literature and Luther in the previous chapter and saw that the Christianity was born in a context of violence. Jesus taught his followers not to retaliate, but to be peacemakers, to love their enemies, and to pray for their persecutors in such circumstances. Montgomery points out that history is "an inquiry focusing on past human experience in a society with a view toward the production of significant and comprehensive narratives embracing human actions and reactions in respect to the whole range of natural, rational and spiritual forces."[1] In the light of Montgomery's definition of history, the researcher carefully examines the problem of violence against Christianity from the time when Christian growth started in the first four centuries of the early church. The early growth of the Christian church was confronted with a systematic attempt to suppress or exterminate Christianity by social pressure to the point of violence.

Violence against Christians began with the action of the Sanhedrin against Peter and John in reprisal for their proclamation of the resurrection of Jesus Christ (Acts 4:1–3, 5). Violence took place at the time of the stoning

1. This definition was given by Professor David Coles during historiography class lecture at Concordia Theological Seminary on 12 March 2012.

of Stephen, following which the Christians of Jerusalem were driven out of the city and scattered in every direction (Acts 8:1–4). Harrison writes that "Diocletian attempted not only to exterminate the Christians, but also to destroy their literature. He confiscated and burned all copies of the Scriptures that he found and demolished the church buildings."[2] Violence characterized the beginning of the church. The Christians were misunderstood by the pagans. They considered Christians to be atheists, anti-social, and politically subversive. Violence was the protest of heathenism against the gospel in its spiritual and social manifestation.[3] So how did Christians respond to violence against them in the first, second, and fourth centuries?

First-Century Response

Johnson notes, "Jesus's response to religious violence of the first century was often ignored, but never forgotten. Even when the church herself persecuted Christian heretics, Jews, and Muslims, some Christians still struggled to bear witness to the peace mandate of their Lord."[4] There are examples available of those who bear witness in circumstances of violence. Johnson further argues that "the Christian religion was spread by violence [by non-Christians] beginning with the apostles and their followers."[5] Hecht notes, "Frequently, early Christians who refused to renounce their faith in Christ literally were fed to the lions. They had no armies and conquered no lands by force in the name of Christianity for centuries after Christ established His church."[6] The Christian church was often subjected to violence.[7] Hornus records a prayer that Clement, an elder in the church at Rome, wrote during Nero's violent attacks against early Christians. Hornus quotes the prayer, "Grant that we may be obedient to your Almighty and Glorious name. You, Master, gave them imperial power through your majestic and indescribable might."[8]

2. Harrison, *Baker's Dictionary of Theology*, 403.
3. Harrison, 403.
4. Johnson, *Peacemaking and Religious Violence*, 2.
5. Hecht, *Two Wars*, 17.
6. Hecht, 17.
7. Hecht, 17.
8. Hornus, *It Is Not Lawful*, 80–81.

Second- and Third-Century Response

Cairns points out that Polycarp, as a faithful cross-bearer, was burned at the stake for refusing to renounce his faith in response to violent acts against him. Cairns maintain that "Polycarp was a valuable witness to the early church even to death."[9] Cairns notes that "the apologists faced a hostile government, which they tried to win with the arguments of their literary productions."[10] Cairns further notes that "They tried to convince the leaders of the state that the Christians had done nothing to deserve the persecutions being inflicted on them."[11] Culliton argues that "the early church was mainly nonviolent and consciously pacifist. No circumstances justified a Christian use of force."[12] "Tertullian demanded a connection between Christian teaching and practical moral life."[13] His philosophy on pacifism has been a subject of debate.[14] Witness for Christ in the midst of violence was common by early Christians. They chose to die for their faith. Hastings, confirms this by writing that "as they persisted in their obduracy Saturninus read out a sentence of execution and the twelve of them, seven men and five women were immediately beheaded.[15] Their witnessing life and their theology of the cross began to give way from the fourth century.

Fourth-Century Response

Windass writes that violent intent started in the fourth century with Constantine after he was successful in a battle by the symbol of the cross.[16] Hurlbut argues that "the declaration of Christianity as the official religion of the Roman Empire developed to just war."[17] Cicero argued that a "holy war waged for revenge or defense could be just."[18] Eusebius of Caesarea,

9. Cairns, *Christianity Through Centuries*, 74–75.
10. Cairns, 105.
11. Cairns, 105.
12. Culliton, *Nonviolence*, 34.
13. Cahill, *Love Your Enemies*, 42.
14. Cahill, 42.
15. Hastings, *A World History of Christianity*, 25.
16. Windass, *Christianity Versus Violence*, 22.
17. Hurlbut, *Story of the Christian Church*, 58–63.
18. Hurlbut, 58–63.

Constantine's bishop and adviser, compelled the laity to wage just wars. The origin of just war tradition is traced to Saint Augustine. Marshall argues, "In the early works, he was concerned with issues of philosophy and culture. But later his interest turned to the defense of Christian life and faith."[19] Augustine's framework for just war theory centers around three guiding principles: (1) just cause; (2) requirement of legitimate authority to wage war; and (3) right intention.[20] Christians responded to religious violence differently at the beginning of early church and during the first through fourth centuries. The researcher examines what current scholarship contributes to how Christians can have insight in response to the problem of religious violence in our society.

Current Literature

Huntington argues that religion is a cause of violence and he maintains that "religion is a central culprit, pointing to the irrational, absolute and divisive character of religious faith, particularly that of extremists or fundamentalists."[21] Pape and Cavanaugh, on the one hand, note that religion plays a major role in international violence and terrorism and that religious fundamentalism or intense faith makes violence more likely and potentially lethal.[22] Barkun opposes connecting religious violence with fundamentalism. Barkun argues that

> attempts to screen religious groups for violence by checking for fundamentalism ignores the fact that both the history of fundamentalism and the practice of the vast majority of contemporary groups identified as fundamentalists are decidedly nonviolent and that the reality is that religious beliefs alone are a poor indicator of any propensity to violence.[23]

19. Marshall, *Restless Heart*, 107.

20. Augustine, *City of God*, xvii–xxxvi.

21. Huntington, *Clash of Civilizations*, 96, 209–11, 254.

22. Pape, *Dying to Win*, 46.

23. Barkun, "Religious Violence," 55–70. David Harrington Watt equally offers similar objections to the misguided understanding of fundamentalism in "The Meaning and End of Fundamentalism," 271–74.

Violent Response

Arnett points out that "conflict is an inevitable moral part of living that cannot and should not be eliminated."[24] However, Arnett maintains that "the common way to deal with conflict in interpersonal relationships is with some form of violence or the violation of another's dignity without being oppressed."[25] Culver, arguing from a nuclear point of view, writes that "pacifist doctrine does not lead to peace but anarchy and chaos, because today's leading pacifists' ideas are often based purely on tradition, and ignoring that in a fallen world, often the only way to peace is through defensive strength."[26] Pilar and Dietmar say, "Much space exists between realism or national security that dismisses all talk on moral restraints in violence as sentimental, and those who in the name of nonviolence or peace deny the possibility of any moral legitimacy to violence."[27] In advocating a just response to violence, Eckhart and Aron argue, "Legitimacy and illegitimacy of using force are to be defined in such a way that they remain open for variations of the divine action."[28] Griffith points out, "Augustine and Ambrose's justification of violence is the reason for current involvement of Christian groups in sectarian violence."[29] The discussion of violence by scholars reveals that there are those who favor a violent response to violence. Others favor the tradition and theology of nonviolence as a Christian resource in the struggle against and in response to violence.

Nonviolent Response

Carter believes that "violence in the Old Testament does not mean God teaches us these days to resolve around armaments that depend on weapons capable of wiping out the human race."[30] Long says, "Rather it should be to promote a general well-being of people to overcome hostility and adopt

24. Arnett, *Dwell in Peace*, 13.
25. Arnett, 13.
26. Culver, *Peace Mongers*, 29.
27. Mieth and Aquino, *Return of Just War*, 89.
28. Eckhart, *Justice through Violence?*, 9. See also Aron, *Century of Total War*, 57.
29. Griffith, *War on Terrorism*, 20–23, 134–35.
30. Carter, *War*, 115–16.

compassion and reconciliation."[31] Haak maintains, "We alone are responsible for controlling this violence. When it is confronted with violence, a society may decide against its use."[32] Daschke and Kille say, "Religion and violence have a complicated relationship to sustain the argument that 'the Bible made me do it.'"[33] Cole writes, "It is because we often approach recent conflicts more on the basis of sustaining Biblically and historically informed moral reflections which advocates just violence position as Biblically sound and morally superior to its rivals."[34] Hengel states that the position of Jesus and the early Christians on the question of violence was radically different from that of the zealots, because Jesus's model of nonviolence demanded that his followers renounce violence and love their enemies.[35]

Vanderhaar supports this view and notes, "The gospels do not portray Jesus as a zealot, eager for the violent overthrow of Roman occupation."[36] Tsetsis points out that for a Christian, the issue at stake is not so much the combat against violence, but the elimination of the things that provoke violence.[37] Irvin insists that one of the principles for reconciliation and peace is a commitment to refuse to sanction violence as a holy act.[38] Hauerwas argues that "Christians are told by our Lord Savior that we must prepare for death because we refuse to kill in the name of survival."[39] Merton[40] and Dear[41] argue that nonviolence is the Christian response to contemporary violence.

De Gruchy[42] and Biggar[43] suggest that forgiveness and reconciliation could help resist, overcome, and recover from violence. Chapman argues that a Christian pastoral theology provides the resources to address the underlying

31. Long, *Peace Thinking*, 98.
32. Haak, "Mapping Violence," 29–30.
33. Daschke and Kille, *A Cry Instead of Justice*, 14.
34. Cole, *When God Says War*, 116.
35. Hengel, *Victory Over Violence*, 88.
36. Vanderhaar, *Christians and Nonviolence*, 53.
37. Tsetsis, "Non-Violence," 61.
38. Irvin, "Terror of History," 53.
39. Hauerwas, "Christian Nonviolence," 246–47.
40. Merton, *Peace in the Post-Christian Era*.
41. Dear, *Living Peace*.
42. De Gruchy, *Reconciliation*.
43. Susin and Aquino, *Reconciliation*.

cause of religious violence.[44] Kreider, Kreider, and Widjaja believe that for Christians, resurrection today can mean that God's power of peace and life has overcome and is overcoming the power of violence and death.[45] Chernus maintains that "even if they should lose their lives, they know that they do so in a winning cause."[46] Thus, Christianity prepared adherents to accept war and other adversity as a necessary part of the intensification of evil which must take place during the end times, just as Jesus had provided the model by accepting his death on the cross.[47]

Observation

The early Christian church was pacifist at the beginning. When Christianity was the official religion of the Roman Empire, Christians saw it as their duty not only to protect her existence, but to protect others. Hence, current views of response to persecution and suffering today do not differ significantly from the early church. Das argues, "Of all human institutions, religion is essentially supranational. Religions have cut across the political, ethnological and linguistic boundaries in all periods of human history."[48] Thus, Midgley quotes Bunyan, "The Christian pilgrimage is not about the race of saints along the way to heaven, or of the dangers and encouragement of the pilgrim, but rather a discussion of the qualifications needed to enter the gate at the end of the journey."[49]

44. Chapman, "Terrorism," 120–37.
45. Kreider, Kreider, and Widjaja, *Culture of Peace*, 140.
46. Chernus, *American Nonviolence*, 96.
47. Chernus, 96.
48. Das, *Shadow of the Cross*, 1.
49. Midgley, *Miscellaneous Works of John Bunyan*, 133–34.

CHAPTER FOUR

Research Design and Method

This research is based on historical resources and interviews. The researcher has employed a qualitative study methodology, which combines historical analysis and phenomenological and descriptive method for this area of study. The research is aimed at examining why some Christians in Northern Nigeria have resorted to violent means in response to the challenges of religious violence. Specific qualitative research measures are then put in place for gathering data through interviews, questionnaires, field research, and participant observation as described by Creswell.[1] Since Brundage suggests that a research design should have "clear, straightforward structures which lead to neutrality,"[2] information was used from interviews, factual available data, and some participant observation, which involves accessing the social world to understand the ways that individuals inhabit and response to issues of life.[3]

Two procedures are important because a methodology could give information that the other may not provide, so through interview and observation a researcher is able to produce an accurate account or data. This is because to write an orderly account of human beings, experiences are by definition interpretive, by which one makes sense of the world and meaning.[4] The task of qualitative research is not to explain the world to all peoples, but to describe reality in ways that enable understanding and actions to be changed. This is what informs Marshall's argument that during in-depth interview studies,

1. See Creswell, *Research Design*.
2. Brundage, *Going to the Sources*, 108.
3. Mowatt and Swinton, *Practical Theology and Qualitative Research*, 29.
4. Mowatt and Swinton, 29.

observation plays an important role.[5] This type of study seeks to qualify results where variables are already clearly defined.[6] At the time of carrying out this research, the researcher lived and traveled among people in Northern Nigeria. Although there were some logistic challenges compared to those who live in a well-ordered and predictable society,[7] linguistic issues can also raise difficulties, especially when ensuring that questions asked carry the same meaning when translated. But the researcher had gainful experience in the use of qualitative method. The selected interviewees, their familiarity with the local language, as well as English and Hausa, and cordial relationships are in accordance with this study because they have provided an enabling environment for the researcher to have direct contact with the people that eliminated bias. This is in consonant with Janvier who explains that a face-to-face culture like Nigeria is a natural setting for doing interviews and discussing opinions verbally as that is how problems traditionally were solved.[8]

Descombe presents three kinds of interviews.[9] He believes that structured interviews involve strict control over the formatted questions and answers. It is like a one-on-one questionnaire. Paton and Bernard say that "qualitative research creates interactive conversation between an interviewer and interviewees, to gain their trust."[10] The semi-structured interview is one in which the interviewer has listed items, and they have flexibility in the order of the questions they are asking to give the opportunity for the participant to present a broader view of answering the questions.[11] Descombe further explains that the unstructured interview is one in which the interviewer introduces the subject and allows the interviewee to form and develop their ideas concerning the trend of thoughts, and the work of the interviewer is just to guide in an open-ended discussion to arrive at objective conclusions.[12] The researcher used both the unstructured interview and open-ended questions to allow

5. Marshall, *Designing Qualitative Research*, 78.

6. Elliston, *Introduction to Missiological Research*, 144–45.

7. The reason is because of an erratic supply of electricity as well as the increasing incidences of violent armed robbery both on homes and while traveling (the researcher himself suffered armed robbery several times and assault along roads twice).

8. Janvier, *How to Write*, 64.

9. Descombe, *Good Research Guide*, 16.

10. Patton, *Qualitative Research*, 1.

11. Bernard, *Research Methods*, 7.

12. Maxwell, *Qualitative Research Design*, 73.

for the flexibility to examine the problem and to help the interviewees gain confidence in the information they gave without manipulation. The interviews were all conducted in English and Hausa, as appropriate.

Limitations

The researcher comes from one of the largest countries in Africa, Nigeria. It is a country with unique challenges, especially with regards to the long-standing religious violence that has created difficulties in accessing primary resources and finances, and new travel restrictions, particularly in Northern Nigeria.

Another challenge that could be perceived as a limitation is that most previous and current researchers have concentrated enormous time and resources researching about the sociopolitical and economic situations and bad governance as the causes for most of the religious violence that occur. Other, especially Christian, researchers have spent their energies researching and making proposals for better relationships between Muslims and Christians in Northern Nigeria. Their focus, however, is limited because there is no prior study done concerning the reason why it appears some Christians in Northern Nigeria have resorted to violent means, especially if their response to religious violence is different from their tradition of pacifism. Thus, this research is both important and challenging because it has to start from the basics relying mainly on secondary sources where available from outside writers rather than from observers who are on site.

A third challenge is that some of the primary witnesses died in religious violence, creating the urgent need to take advantage of available witnesses who are alive for researching the problem of religious violence. The fourth challenge was limitation of finances to perform the study (the researcher undertook this study program while on leave without pay, experiencing financial stress). A final limitation was that some of the participants found it difficult to make travel plans to the designated locations for interviews because of the severe terrain.

Delimitations

The researcher depended mainly on the data he collected from participants during the field research. His wide-ranging experiences in the various roles he served in ministry throughout sub-Saharan Africa aided him a great deal in the research. Some of the participants had been students under the researcher in seminary, others were members of the churches the researcher served, and others were people the researcher met when he was presenting papers around Northern Nigeria on how to curtail religious violence. This group of people expressed deep appreciation for the research project. The burden for this research began after 2001 when religious violence broke out in the Kaduna and Kano states.

The researcher could not initially undertake the project on account of his writing *Forgiving from the Heart*.[13] This book was intended to contribute toward healing members in the body of Christ from the hurt caused by religious violence. The researcher was supported by individual Christians and two churches from Northern Nigeria in order to carry out this project, and they offered their full cooperation toward making this work a success. The researcher, however, did not extend his work across the geographical cities of Nigeria due to the costs involved. The researcher limited the research plan to thirteen cities of Northern Nigeria. This policy was in keeping with the wise counsel that Descombe gives: "Because of limited resources, the researcher should not stretch his area of interview across a large geographical area to avoid incurring prohibitive costs."[14]

Research Questions and Operational Questions

In order to understand the answer to the question why some Christians in Northern Nigeria have resorted to violent means in response to religious violence, it will help to establish an understanding of what factors motivated them to ignore the practice of Christian living and pacifism. Four research questions were identified.

Research Question 1: What was the social and religious context in which the Christian church in Northern Nigeria was planted?

Operational Questions:

1. How do they describe their social context?
2. How do they describe their religious context?

13. Dadang, *Forgiving from the Heart*.

14. Descombe, *Good Research Guide*, 165.

Research Question 2: How do Christians in Northern Nigeria describe what the Christian message means to them?

Operational Questions:

1. How do they describe their previous religious background?
2. How do they describe their previous conversion experience?
3. How do they describe their conversion experience?
4. How do they describe their conversion location?

Research Question 3: What do Christians in Northern Nigeria describe the cause(s) of religious violence?

Operational Questions:

1. Who is the cause of religious violence?
2. What impact does religious violence have on them?
3. What impact does religious violence have on the church?

Research Question 4: What solution to the problem of religious violence do Christians in Northern Nigeria propose?

Operational Questions:

1. How do they personally experience religious violence?
2. How do they relate biblical teaching to their problem?
3. What solution(s) do they propose to religious violence?

Introduction to the Field Research Findings

In the preliminary research done on this subject, before the interviews were conducted, the researcher did a pilot study with thirty Christians in Northern Nigeria in order to form the basis for completing the research work by means of interviews.[15] Those interviewed were baptized congregational members who were actively involved in church fellowship groups and communicant members. The pilot study helped to set the base for the interview protocol. The responses also revealed that the participants understood what the researcher was examining. It further helped the researcher to reorganize and reframe some of the research questions. There were four additional factors

15. The preliminary research began with a pilot study with seven respondents from February 2001 to December 2009. It was the month in which another episode of major religious violence broke out in Kaduna. He further devoted a substantial amount of time from June through December 2013.

that compelled the researcher to promote his interest in conducting this qualitative research project.

The first reason was the researcher's experience as country director, coordinating field responsibility among religious leaders across denominations in Northern Nigeria. The second reason was the researcher's relationship in ministry with those who are in pastoral positions and lay leaders from parachurch organizations who had the ability to share their views on religious violence in Northern Nigeria. The third reason was the random selection of those people who are independently involved in reaching people of other faiths with the good news and had been involved in ministering in violent communities. The fourth reason was the random selection of those who had personally experienced religious violence and whose friends, coworkers, and relatives had been killed, and/or property (such as house) burned or destroyed, and/or people who narrowly escaped religious violence as through fire.

Description of the Participants Respondents

Personal interviews were conducted with eighty-four Christians randomly selected, seven participants each from thirteen states. However, seven died in religious violence before their planned interviews. Thirty participants were already interviewed during the pilot in 2001 and from June to December 2013. Table 1 shows the number of participants in each of the states in Nigeria.

The breakdown of the respondents randomly selected was done by district church leaders who are clergy themselves. The district leaders were requested to ask the pastors to select baptized congregational members from their church membership registration lists.[16] The congregational members chosen by the pastors were those whose membership numbers on the registration lists were eleven, seventeen, twenty-three, twenty-nine, and thirty-five. The demographic data of the respondents showed that out of the eighty-five interviewees, seventeen were laymen and fifteen were laywomen. Three were Evangelical Missionary Society missionaries.[17] Fourteen were widows of the

16. District leaders are next in ranking to national leaders, and they exercise authority over the pastor's place over their congregations. They also provide supervision for the smooth running of the church denomination.

17. The Evangelical Missionary Society is the mission department of the Evangelical Church Winning All, which has 1600 couples serving as missionaries around the African continent.

Table 1: Number of Participants in Each State.

States	Participants
Bauchi	7
Borno	6
Gombe	7
Jigawa	6
Jos	8
Kano	7
Kaduna	7
Katsina	6
Kebbi	6
Niger	6
Sokoto	6
Yobe	6
Zamfara	6

martyred from religious violence. Thirteen were from two para-church organizations that have tried to build bridges toward interreligious relationships. Eleven were youth leaders from various church congregations. Five were from secondary school, university, or those who had attained some level of graduate school. Four were market traders who did not have formal education, and three were Muslim background believers.[18] The geographical location of the interviewees mentioned above were from twelve states of Northern Nigeria plus one from the central or Middle Belt where Christians have experienced religious violence. The researcher, who had served as the former general secretary of the Evangelical Church Winning All, earned popularity and integrity before the district leaders, who made the interviewing environment conducive for him by ensuring that it was safe for both him and the participants who were traveling from other towns to the venue of the interviews. The researcher's personal assistant, a professional journalist, was very useful in all the places we traveled. He provided clear explanations to interviewees and recorded all responses coherently.

18. Muslim background believers or MBBs are those who came to faith from Islamic backgrounds.

However, some problems were encountered in the period slated for carrying out the research field work. The first difficulty was that the rains are heavier from the months of June until around the end of October in most parts of Nigeria. This made travel difficult and prevented or delayed some of the participants from turning up at the venues of the interviews. A second challenge was uncertain security situations, especially in places like Borno, Yobe, Bauchi, and Kano, as a result of the Boko Haram random bombings of places of worship. The researcher had to keep changing meeting places and rescheduling interviews for the safety of both the interviewees, the researcher, and his personal assistant. Indeed, the third challenge was the constant absence of electrical power, and so, at some instances, candles or lamps were used during interviews. A practical experience that was worth documenting in qualitative research was the deaths of five family members of the ECWA during the interview exercise. Their deaths were as a result of religious violence that broke out shortly before the researcher's arrival to their community.

The situation required the researcher to have to take a considerable amount of time during their moment of sober reflection with those of them who lost their loved ones to provide trauma counseling rather than going ahead with his interviews as planned.[19] However, from all indications, the travels were a worthwhile venture. The interviewees appreciated the opportunity to share their stories and the subject of this work being addressed. They gave the researcher and his personal assistant their maximum cooperation. The qualitative data that was collected from interviewees was transcribed, analyzed, and categorized in relation to the questions of the research. Areas that were not related to the main guiding questions of the research were sorted and set aside, prior to sifting through all the information gathered from the field work. In every category, respondents' responses were further re-categorized according to their relevant responses. For instance, responses could be subdivided between those of lay church members and those from para-church organizations. In every interviewees' responses, each question answered was analyzed by the researcher before categorizing the answers into headings that show themselves out naturally from the respondents' answers.

19. Healing the wounds of trauma is a step that helps people understand and experience God's healing and occurs best in their heart language, and this particularly seeks to help church leaders who have members in their churches who have been traumatized.

They were grouped in relation to the guiding or operational questions for the research. The researcher coded citations in this work to protect the identity of the respondents.

CHAPTER FIVE

Research Findings and Analysis

The research questions for this study were clustered into four main groups: (1) social and religious context, (2) religious background and conversion experience, (3) causes of religious violence, and (4) possible solutions to the problem of religious violence. While the first two sets of research questions were used primarily to help classify the participants in the study, the last two questions were designed to focus on what the participants thought should be their responses given their exposure to religious violence.

Research Question One: Social and Religious Context

The first research question was, "What was the social and religious context in which Christians in Northern Nigeria were planted?" Findings show that the majority (72.2 percent) of the respondents agreed there was cordial coexistence and mutual respect for human dignity. The respondents claimed that Muslims, Christians, and those who practiced traditional religion coexisted well with each other in every community. The next highest percentage (22.2 percent) agreed that these groups showed respect for human life, and the last group of respondents (5.6 percent) expressed some degree of social hostility. Many described the social context in which they were planted.

Operational Question 1: Previous Social Context

Many responses indicate a previously peaceful situation between Christians and Muslims. A respondent remarked, "I have lived in the city of Kaduna for over forty years. Life for us was peaceful. We respected each other's religions" (ASUB13).[1] Another respondent remarked, "Our relationships with other people here in Katsina were very good and cordial. In fact as a hair dresser, I treated all my customers equally," (LIYD14).[2] Another respondent commented, "I came from the south to Kano in 1960 to do business. I had good business friends who were Hausa Muslims. We cordially traded together, and we made profit. As trusted business partners, we progressed in our businesses" (ASAM19).[3] Yet another interviewee said,

> Life was enjoyable here in Zaria and the rest part of Northern Nigeria. I did my national youth service corps here. I met a beautiful Hausa Christian and I married her. On our wedding day, both Muslims and Christians' relatives turned in mass. It was one of my most memorable social gatherings that recorded my diary. (JMNA20)[4]

Others commented on a more negative social context. One person said, "There seems to be gradual social disparity against non-Muslims groups here in Zamfara state. We see that our Christian communities are ignored development; social amenities such as providing clean drinking water. Schools are tactfully denied for Christian children to attend" (IRIS17).[5] Another individual commented,

> We cry out every time on how governments in Northern Nigeria favor Islam over those of us who are of other religious groups. This social hostility has distorted our peaceful sociocultural and religious diversity. We see social hostility in religious discrimination. We are denied equal rights to employment; acquire lands to build churches; our children are denied school, and we Christians are denied promotion in government offices in Northern Nigeria. (BAKN06)[6]

1. Interview Mon5Mar01.
2. Interview Thu8Mar01.
3. Interview Fri30Mar01.
4. Interview Sat31Mar01.
5. Interview Sun 1Apr01.
6. Interview Thu12Apr01.

Operational Question 2: Previous Religious Context

Findings demonstrate that 94.4 percent of the respondents faced religious intolerance from Muslim hostility and British officials. The respondents' views showed the preferential orientation continued when the British withdrew and independence was granted. It gave the Muslims freedom to advance the cause of Islam at the expense of those of them who came to Christian faith.

The remarks of respondents are represented by the following response:

> Those of us who were converted from Islam to Christianity have faced severe persecution. We are aware that even the relationships of missionaries who brought us to spiritual growth with British authority also remained difficult with us. When we started work as Native Authority clerks, we were not trusted as office workers by both British officials and Muslims. (BRAU04)[7]

One of the respondents, a Hausa man, reported how he had a good relationship with his Muslim friends during religious festivals. "I had a good relationship with all my Muslim friends. At Christmas, we all gathered to celebrate and ate together as a family. When it was Sallah period, they also invited me to share in their joy" (AUMA05).[8]

However, a note of caution was sounded by another interviewee, who said, "I observed the peace we knew initially, was a temporal one. Muslims exercised control since the British Indirect Rule compounding it with religion aided radical Islamic propaganda over that of the Christian faith affecting all religious groups who are non-Muslims in Northern Nigeria" (ANOM73).[9]

Research Question Two: How Do Christians in Northern Nigeria Describe What the Christian Message Means to Them?

The next research question was, "What was the religious experience of Christians before their conversion?" It was designed to help determine what

7. Interview Thu19Apr01.
8. Interview Sun22Apr01.
9. Interview Mon23Apr01.

were the religious backgrounds and loyalties of the interviewees prior to their becoming Christians.

Operational Question 1: Religious Loyalty Prior to Conversion to Christianity

The first operational question was designed to have the interviewees describe what their religious background was prior to coming to Christianity. The majority (93.4 percent) of those interviewed had no previous loyalties with Christianity. They shared the religious foundation of animism as found in the African continent. The next highest (5.6 percent) represented a group that had originated from a syncretistic form of Islam mixed with traditional animism. The remaining 1 percent represented a syncretistic religious background.

Findings demonstrate that the majority of the respondents described their religious backgrounds in terms of religious beliefs that recognized spirits controlling the physical world. The majority of the respondents described their previous cultic fraternity with the power of mana.[10] The majority of respondents presupposed that through their diligent sacrifice and compliance with the taboos, they make peace with the spirits to retain the power. The main benefit of this fraternity as reported by the majority of respondents was personal acquisition of power to confront any warring opponent. This worldview reports receiving visits by deceased family members. One area that the majority of respondents reported was spiritual power possession as a means to respond to religious violence. Thus, it was highly sought after by the majority of them, who described themselves as previously controlled by a spiritual power. These situations resulted in what the majority of respondents described as a means by which religious violence could end.

In traditional religion, Steinbronn rightly writes,

> Following the Supreme God is a host of lesser gods. These gods possess specific powers. Some gods exercise power over human

10. Mana is "a supernatural force or power that may be ascribed to persons, spirits, or inanimate objects. Mana may be either good or evil, beneficial or dangerous. The term was first used in the 19th century in the West during debates concerning the origin of religion. It was first used to describe what apparently was interpreted to be an impersonal, amoral, supernatural power that manifested itself in extraordinary phenomena and abilities. Anything distinguished from the ordinary (e.g., an uncommonly shaped stone) is so because of the mana it possesses." See "Mana," *Encyclopedia Britannica*, http://www.britannica.com/EBchecked/topic/361194/mana.

> beings. In addition to spirit beings, there exists in the external world a power called mana. Mana can be possessed and it can also be made to adhere in objects such as charms or medicines.[11]

African religion is power controlled. Okorocha writes, "The religiousness of any belief system in Africa is measured in terms of its mana context and its visibility in terms of its mana effect."[12] Okorocha continues, "The missiological import of all this is that the African believes a religion to be useful and worthy of profession only if it embodies and imports power. Otherwise, it is rejected and a more powerful alternative is sought."[13] He goes on to say, "Power encounters are necessary within African religious systems. For the African, everything is about power. This was especially relevant for many of the early converts to Christianity."[14]

Okorocha writes, "As a model of religious change, African conversion may be described as a case of power encounter in terms of a confrontation between two or several systems of salvation, resulting in a conscious and radical movement on the part of people in the direction of power."[15]

Operational Question 2: Experience Prior to Conversion

The second operational question was designed to have the interviewees describe their religious experience prior to conversion to Christianity. The findings demonstrate that before their conversion the majority (40.6 percent) of the respondents described their lives as fearful; they constantly sought to appease the spirits of their gods to remain under protection. The next highest (21.6 percent) was an inward fear of the unknown. When they found themselves in trouble, fear threw the respondents into uncertainty exclaiming that the gods had forsaken them! Following this are (14.9 percent) respondents who struggled with their personal sin. Constantly one, if not both, of these phenomenal situations were described.

11. Steinbronn, *Worldviews*, 55.
12. Okorocha, "Religious Conversion in Africa," 168–70.
13. Okorocha, 174.
14. Okorocha, 174.
15. Okorocha, 175–76.

The respondents narrated their pre-conversion experience as being full of the struggle with fear of the unknown. The following expressions represent pre-conversion views expressed by one of the respondents: "Before I was converted, I always had fear of the unknown, because my traditional religion did not seem to give me assurance of my future life. I lived in constant fear. Nevertheless, I did not listen to threat of my thoughts. I decided to become a Christian" (EMAS29).[16] Another respondent remarked, "Before I was converted, there was a particular spirit that came to me at night warning me not convert to any other faith. Otherwise I would lose the power given me and die" (DROW22).[17]

A custodian to the shrine remarked, "Before my conversion, I struggled inside me between becoming a Christian and remained the husband of two wives and four concubines as tradition allowed" (SWAM31).[18] Another respondent narrated, "I am the only son to my father. He passed the tradition of ancestral worship to me. In addition to the requirement to keep the oath I took to preserve it to the next generation; I was expected to keep the legacy and pass it on to my eldest son. I was afraid to convert. But I had to make a decision" (DRAJ28).[19]

These circumstances continued among the majority of respondents. Every one of them recounted a similar encounter that is based on spiritual phenomenon. The next largest group of respondents (21.9 percent) described their conversion. "What I felt before my conversion was lack of peace of mind and lack of sleep," said one interviewee (JGWA81).[20] In each of these situations, the respondents described some form of internal conflict before conversion. Many of the respondents continue to relate their experiences into their answers provided in the next question.

16. Interview Sat05May01.
17. Interview Sat12May01.
18. Interview Sat19May01.
19. Interview Sat26May01.
20. Interview Sat14Apr01.

Operational Question 3: Details of Conversion to Christianity

The third operational question was as follows: "Describe clearly the location of your conversion. When did your conversion happen? Please, explain to me about your experience. Where were you: church, home, village?" The purpose for this operational question three progressed from the previous religious background and context toward the real events surrounding the phenomenon of conversion.

The majority interviewed (37.5 percent) described interacting with missionaries and cross-cultural evangelism outside the church as the how and where they were converted. This was overwhelmingly true of those who had described themselves as previously involved in traditional religion. The next largest responses (25.6 percent) came from respondents who were uncertain of the location of their conversion. The church was the second most significant location (18.8 percent) identified by the respondents. Their personal residence (15.6 percent) was the other frequently cited location of conversion. The data establish that the majority of those who experienced a conversion (58.2 percent) did so outside of the church building. The data establish that the missionaries conducted their operations primarily in the field, which is to say where the people live and work.

Operational Question 4: Analyses of Conversion Experience

The purpose of this question is to describe the events that surrounded the phenomena of the conversion experience. The majority of the respondents fell within three categories of conversion experience. They described either a desire for deep repentance (34.9 percent) or a sense of peace, confidence, and freedom (32.6 percent). The third category of respondents (20.6 percent) was not sure of when conversion occurred.

The following responses are associated with the first two groups: "I saw in my dream a man dressed in white clothes. The brightness in my room was like the shining of the stars. I was afraid. I was looking for a place to hide my face. Then I heard a voice, 'Fear not, for I am with you, come to Jesus'" (BWUR08).[21] Another interviewee said, "I was born to a Christian home.

21. Interview Fri23Nov01.

Every morning I heard my mother singing Christian choruses and reading the Bible at our devotions. That Christian virtue brought me to conversion and I found peace of heart" (CRIN09).[22] A third participant said, "When I became converted, I got a new heart and I was a sign to all my family members. God's power freed me from the bondage of Satan" (AMCR43).[23]

For some, the conversion experience involved more of a change than for others. One interviewee said,

> I hated pastors and evangelists. I did not want to walk near the church or attend any either. I did not want them to talk to me about Jesus. But I eventually converted. Now I do not only desire constant church fellowship, but I have plans to support their ministry. (DYNG65)[24]

Another commented, "I was very violent and could not show mercy to anyone in my community. I experienced a wonderful release and happiness following my conversion. I now enjoy company with community members and I have good relationship with people" (TIYL21).[25] A third responded, "I lived a life of bitterness and lack of forgiveness. When I was converted, peace and forgiveness fill my life. I experienced a change in my life as I trusted Jesus" (DBEM90).[26] After their conversion experience, many of the respondents described the release from bondage brought about by worship of spirits. Respondents interviewed identified freedom, peace, and trust as outcomes of their conversion into the Christian faith.

Thus, Gill suggests that the "Biblical gospel is not that humans can save themselves inwardly or that whatever happens outwardly is meant to be, but rather that a personal God loves them and that with divine help, they can freely love others."[27] Human beings are not God, but humans can participate in the grace manifest in Christ and being forgiven by God, both give and receive joy.[28] Walther comments that

---

22. Interview Fri30Nov01.
23. Interview Wed7Nov01.
24. Interview Wed28Nov01.
25. Interview Sun15Jul01.
26. Interview Sun22Jul01.
27. Gill, *Cambridge Companion*, 61.
28. Gill, 61.

> the Gospel does not require anything good that man must furnish: not a good heart, not a good disposition, no improvement of his conditions, no godliness, and no love either of God or men. It issues no orders, but it changes man. It plants love into his heart and makes him capable of all good works. It demands nothing, but gives all.[29]

Research Question Three: Causes of Religious Violence

The third research question was, "How do Christians in Northern Nigeria describe the cause of religious violence?" This question was designed to identify how religious violence originated and the impact of this violence both for the community and the individual.

Operational Question 1: Cause(s) of Religious Violence

The majority of the respondents (64 percent) described differences in religion to be cause for religious violence. The next highest percentage of responses (16.4 percent) described politics, then economic situation, (9.8 percent), and others ethnic causes (4.1 percent). The last category of responses (3.2 percent) described a lack of discipleship in both Islam and Christianity to be cause for religious violence and (1.6 percent) respondents described God allowing violence to chastise the church.

The following responses are representative of the respondents. One interviewee said, "I know of many prominent Muslim politicians in Northern Nigeria take advantage of religious violence, poverty, and ignorance of the average people to cause destruction with the expectation that when the crises of violence calm down, they reap the dividend of their plan" (BADG43).[30] This was also agreed to by those who are Muslim background believers. They said,

> As a Muslim background believer, I am aware that some of these leaders seemed primarily motivated by their personal desire for

29. Walther, *Proper Distinction*, 16.
30. Interview Sun29Jul01.

> power and others by their own religious zeal. After all, in Islam, there is no distinction between religion and politics. Muslims believe that the Islamic faith should provide the context within which politics operates. (GUBU00)[31]

Others agreed with these concerns. One interviewee said,

> In Northern Nigeria, everything is about religion and at the slightest conflict, it always turns violent. I observe for years that in the entire country Islam is the only favored religion. Otherwise, why has Islam become so intolerant to the extent she suppresses non-Muslims provoking them always? Religion is the cause for violence. (ALWO34)[32]

Another participant stated,

> We as Christians in Northern Nigeria do not organize ourselves like the Muslims, because our religion does not teach us to plan to kill people in their sleep. But we are thrown into confusion, sorrows, and despair today because of Islamic propaganda that any who is not a Muslim should die by the sword. For years now, Islam has used religion to cause religious violence on non-Muslims. (KWDU5)[33]

Other causes cited for religious violence included the following interviewee's response, "I am thinking God has allowed religious violence toward Christians to purify them for not evangelizing the Muslims. Otherwise, while have we been praying, burning and killing Christians has not stopped. Maybe it is our disobedience responsible for religious violence" (SMUA10).[34] Yet another respondent said, "We know one of the facts causing religious violence in Northern Nigeria is economic disparity between the rich and poor. Many of us have finished universities in the past five years, yet we remain unemployed. But we see new buildings are constructed daily by the rich people" (AOSN03).[35]

---

31. Interview Wed4Apr01.
32. Interview Wed11Apr01.
33. Interview Wed18Apr01.
34. Interview Wed25Apr01.
35. Interview Sun2Sep01.

Politics as a cause of religious violence is noted in the following respondent's comments,

> I was traveling from Kaduna to Kano in a public transport. Two Muslim politicians were discussing a strategy of how to sponsor religious violence. They keep a pool of poor, unemployed, and illiterate youth [*almajirai*] who are easily bought over to cause religious violence because usually the *almajirai* do not have fixed home addresses. They discussed hired and paid mercenaries from neighboring countries to cause religious violence. (MSES89)[36]

Operational Question 2: Impact of Religious Violence

The majority of the respondents (77.3 percent) described religious violence as having a negative impact on them, and that living in such a brutal environment compelled a Christian to respond to violence with violence. The next highest percent of respondents (11.9 percent) described segregating themselves from living with Muslims, and the third group (10.7 percent) described suspicion against Muslims.

The following represents the impact on the respondents:

> Those of us Christians from Kano know that one major impact of religious violence on us is the spread of Hausa culture, language and oppression has affected our experiences negatively. The trade language and compulsory teaching of Hausa in all Schools in Kano is in itself discriminative. Violence against us has prevented and our children from Western education. Our children cannot attain the required requirements to study at universities. The preferential treatment of Muslims has caused the relegation of non-Muslims in Northern Nigerian to a second-class status, because of the claim that Muslims are greater in number than non-Muslims, and this results in anti-Christian

36. Interview Sun9Sep01.

> discrimination by Muslims, leading to religious violence in Northern Nigeria. (HDAU24)[37]

Others also point to the consequences of religious violence. One interviewee said, "Sir, we thank you for visiting us at the hospital. We are in the hospital as a result of injuries we sustained from last week's religious violence, for which you served as trauma counselor to families whose loved ones were killed. If we did not flee for our lives we would have died" (KAUM30).[38] Another person commented,

> We live in a typically violent environment of Northern Nigeria, and we do not know when this wickedness of religious violence that causes all emotional stress will leave us. This ugly situation has compelled Christians to participate in violent responses to the Muslims. Otherwise, Christians may be eliminated, and leave no Christian to take the gospel to those still outside the church. (TURN48)[39]

Many interviewees commented on the personal emotional impact of violence. One person noted,

> There is constant disruption of peace almost every now and then in Northern Nigeria. I find it very hard to cope with the impact religious violence. I find it too hard to depend on the power of God in the midst of this constant uncertainty, confusion, and despair the menace of religious war is causing on our Christian faith today. (SACH72)[40]

Another respondent said,

> It is not intentional that I have developed so much hatred for the Muslims. I am forced because I am emotionally upset with their actions against Christians. The impact of killing has made me think as if Islam is a blood-seeking religion. This has forced every Christian home to live in daily fear and sorrow. (WALY11)[41]

---

37. Interview Tus24Apr01.
38. Interview Sun16Sep01.
39. Interview Sun23Sep01.
40. Interview Sun30Sep01.
41. Interview Fri5Oct01.

A third participant noted the change in relations between Christians and Muslims when he said,

> We are segregated from each other across towns, cities, villages, and even markets between Christians and Muslims. Muslims whom we have sheltered have turned against us. Muslims hunt for us like bush meat. We grieve and mourn the loss of our loved ones; of jobs, homes, possessions, and opportunities in church and prayer meetings. (AKVN12)[42]

Thus, there were a variety of personal responses to religious violence.

Operational Question 3: Personal Experience of Religious Violence

The majority of the respondents (78.6 percent) personally experienced religious violence against themselves. The next highest group of respondents (28.6 percent) described husbands, wives, or relatives who had been killed. There were also respondents (15.7 percent) who knew of friends and office colleagues who had been killed. Another category of respondents (12.8 percent) described having narrowly escaped death, and others (8.6 percent) had personal loss of property, burning of their own churches, and loss of lives. Thus, most of the interviewees had experienced religious violence firsthand.

Steinbronn writes, "For the Muslim, the world is divided into two realms. One realm is called Dar al-Islam and refers to the community subject to Islam and obedient to Muhammad's message. All others are the disobedient, the infidels, and become the Dar al-Harb, which means 'the house of war.'"[43] This becomes the justification for radical Muslims to seek to kill Christians and to subjugate them.

The following responses are typical of personal experiences of religious violence. A Christian religious knowledge teacher at a government secondary school remarked,

> The government watches terrorists destroying hundreds of churches in my state, along with the killing of 488 Christians. This left only eight Christians including me. You cannot even

42. Interview Fri12Oct01.

43. Steinbronn, *Worldviews*, 52.

> tell who will be the next person to die. Boko Haram published an ultimatum telling Christians to leave Northern Nigeria in three days or face death. In another episode of religious violence in Borno, three hundred and forty-two Christians were killed, and five churches were demolished. Why should I forgive these people? (LRIA15)[44]

Another person commented,

> I am surrounded by the spiritual death of Islam. The Muslims came to kill us, and they shouted, "*Ala-hukabar*," "*Arna kawai*" [mere infidels]. I knew physical death was coming to us. Before I came out of the bedroom, I heard the agony my husband was passing through. They killed him. I quickly smuggled our two-year-old son, and I escaped with him through window [tears running down her cheeks]. Today, God spared me to tell you my story. I know my husband is with Christ. (HRIA91)[45]

Another respondent said, "I am hurt because my younger brother and his wife were killed" (PANG23).[46] Still another Christian said, "Muslims killed my brother and sister in religious violence" (NBAM55).[47]

The experience of three other interviewees is summarized by the following comment, "I narrowly escaped being killed three times. I was returning from a preaching assignment. I ran into Muslim mob. I did not dress in my clergy gown. I dressed like a Muslim still they did not pass me until I recited the *shahāda* [Muslim Creed]. The other two instances were during official travels."[48]

A respondent remarked, "There has been fierce religious violence against Christians in Dogo Nahawa town. Many Christians have been killed, (women and children, as well as men), and over four hundred Christians in that community were almost wiped out" (BDOC87).[49] Another respondent remarked "I have one thousand six hundred and fifty names and addresses of all the

44. Interview Thu5Nov09.
45. Interview Thu12Nov09.
46. Experience of Tus23Dec12.
47. Interview Thu12Nov09.
48. Experience of Tus20Feb01; Sat3Mar01; Sun25Nov08.
49. Interview Tus7Apr09.

Christians killed in Kano by Muslim violence" (ASAN74).[50] Thus, the violence of Muslims in Northern Nigeria is not just personal, but is targeted at groups and villages of Christians.

Operational Question 4: Impact of Religious Violence on the Church

Of the respondents, 35 percent stated that Pentecostal doctrine has entered the church over time. Fifteen percent of the respondents described ecumenical union with other churches as a significant impact on the church. Ten percent of the respondents described an emphasis on numerical growth as a significant impact on the church.

The following responses represent the respondents' descriptions. A second-generation Christian remarked,

> For a time we were overly concerned with the nationalization that surrounded us. In our concern for the development of the church, we tended to lose sight of the unreached peoples and the uncompleted task. We also lost sight of the legacy of the sound gospel passed from missionaries to us. We did not prepare the converts handed to us. We failed to equip them enough. This weakness exposed us to Pentecostals infiltrating the church. (PYUR44)[51]

A women's fellowship leader remarked,

> Increasing church association with other churches created an inter-denominational organization called New Life for All. Its breaking down denominational barriers was one of the foundations on which Pentecostalism was later built. Greater numbers and ecumenical union among churches was a threat to traditional Muslim elites. People from traditional religion converted to Christianity combined with Pentecostal way of preaching, and this further threatened the authority of Muslim-dominated Northern Nigeria, triggering religious violence. (BSBO16)[52]

50. Interview Tus14Apr09.
51. Interview Thu19Nov09.
52. Interview Thu12Nov09.

Another respondent remarked, "I regret Pentecostalism arose from local innovations of a response to spiritual movements where our non-Pentecostal missionaries had already labored in planting churches in Northern Nigeria. Unfortunately, rapid conversion increased religious violence against Christians" (DYKA40).[53]

A youth leader said,

> We sought to train and mobilize every member of participating churches to systematically witness to every non-Christian in their neighborhood and also evangelize through evangelistic teams to non-evangelized areas. It was supported by extensive use of prayer groups, widespread literature distribution, publicity, evangelistic rallies, and church parades by the Boy's Brigade, as well as by radio programs and recordings. (ASH45)[54]

However, there was a lack of depth in these methods. Another respondent remarked,

> The growth in large numbers failed to raise major missiological questions. How were millions of converts to be equipped and taught? As they were converted by lay evangelists, how were they formed into congregations? How was pastoral care handled for such a great number of converts from traditional religious backgrounds or from Islam? How would the converts acquire theological education to help them differentiate Biblical teaching from traditional beliefs? (PEIS26)[55]

The majority of respondents, then, saw that rapid church growth had led to the increasing influence upon numerical growth, without paying attention to the discipleship of those who had been converted, and this led to a rise in Pentecostalism. This, in turn, led to fear on the part of the Muslim leaders and the rise of religious violence.

53. Interview Thu19Nov09.

54. Interview Thu19Nov09.

55. Interview Thu19Nov09.

Research Question Four: Solutions to the Problem of Religious Violence in Northern Nigeria

Operational Question 1: Relating Biblical Response to Violence

The majority of respondents (48.3 percent) described the implications of loving enemies in context of religious war. The next largest response (21.6 percent) described the biblical teaching of loving one's enemies, and another group of respondents (11.6 percent) described praying as a response. A smaller number (3.3 percent) of respondents described forgiveness and one respondent described developing friendship as means to counter religious violence.

The following responses represent the respondents' descriptions. One individual commented, "I know it is another thing to suffer injustice and violation of my Christians right to practice my religion. To deny this fundamental human right to freedom of religion forcefully by another religious group is unacceptable" (ABCK57).[56] Another respondent remarked,

> I see Christians who are struggling with the right response to religious violence as torn between their natural desire for justice and the traditional teaching regarding loving one's enemies as in the teaching of Jesus Christ. Yet, I wrestle in my mind when fresh religious violence against Christians in Northern Nigeria keeps occurring. This always renews hostility and distrust toward those same enemies the Bible teaches we must love. It is hard for me to understand. (CANG88)[57]

Another respondent remarked,

> We know the Christian obligation to love and forgive my Muslims neighbors for the violence committed against Christians. We are always in search to see if Muslims and Christians could end religious violence in Northern Nigeria by advocating for creating peace committees. But this peace initiatives failed as the

56. Interview Sun10Oct04.
57. Interview Sun17Oct04.

> Muslims always had a hidden agenda after such peace committee meetings. (ZBUM76)[58]

Another person said,

> Initially, we thought Christians were facing persecution. We thought to ourselves no matter which way we fight back we will be defeated unless we reconnected to our source of power Jesus Christ. So we returned to God and resorted to sincere relationship in Christ. We adopted and related a biblical response to violence with an atmosphere of calmness, prayerfulness, fasting and crying for God's intervention. (DEMR82).[59]

Still another respondent remarked,

> We sustained prayer with advocacy for government to stop Muslims from provoking violence against Christians. But government did not do anything to stop violence against Christians. We remained faithful to our biblical principles of the nonviolent and trustworthy God. We reminded ourselves the Bible teaches us to repay evil with good and leave vengeance to God [Rom 12:17–20]. We continued to pray and fast, and had confidence in God for deliverance. God did not deliver us. We are thrown into a state of despair and worry for nonintervention. (ZSUA67)[60]

An additional interviewee remarked,

> We think we are fighting a religious war of persecution, and Muslims are the enemies. Since we are in a religious war, the language of love and forgiveness is not relevant unless warring parties are ready to lay down their instruments of war, so that the violence may stop. It is the tension of religious violence which decreases interest in taking the gospel of love to Muslims. (BDLE54)[61]

58. Interview Sun24Oct04.
59. Interview Sun31Oct04.
60. Interview Sat6Nov04.
61. Interview Sat13Nov04.

A final participant commented, "We encourage Christians to have nothing to do with Muslims because their religion is violent. We also encourage our Christian families to stay away from Muslims' friendship. There is a major religious war between Muslims and Christians, and showing love does not fit our situation with Muslims" (TAYI25).[62]

Thus, while Christians identify the need to love their enemies according to biblical teaching, they find it difficult to do so in the face of recurring religious violence.

Operational Question 2: Solutions to Religious Violence

The majority of respondents (95.2 percent) stated that the solution to religious violence in Northern Nigeria was based on the use of self-defense in response. The majority of respondents considered the ongoing religious violence as a major threat not only to themselves, families, property, and churches, but to Christianity generally. The second group of respondents (3.5 percent) described the use of traditional power as means of additional response to religious violence, and the last group of respondents (2 percent) was undecided. The following responses represent the respondents' descriptions.

For example, one respondent remarked,

> There are no more cheeks left to turn. We have turned both the right and left cheeks for them to slap, and we do not have a third cheek to give, and so we face it. We avenge on the basis of our doctrine of "no third slap." When we applied the Bible to turn our cheeks, it provided for only two slaps. After the second slap, the Bible is silent, and, therefore, we avenge on the basis of that silence. (LMIA39)[63]

Another Christian remarked, "The steady violent attacks have thrown Christians into great confusion. We have advocated for calm and prayer. We do the best we could to make Muslims understand we do not hate them. Yet they follow us to our homes and churches to kill us. This has compelled

62. Interview Sat20Nov04.

63. Interview Wed21Feb01.

us and other Christians to self-defense" (SNLA66).[64] Another respondent commented, "We have implemented the principles of social services in both Christian and Muslim communities. We provided clean drinking water, clinics and hospitals as acts of mercy. Yet they have committed violence against us. We are weary of the incessant religious violence and the constant fear of the Muslim *almajirai*. This forced us to adopt self-defense" (ITAD75).[65]

A respondent remarked on the situation of religious violence in Northern Nigeria. She said, "Many of us Christians in Northern Nigeria have resorted to violent means in response to religious violence because of our traditional African worldview of resisting our enemies by retaliation. Christians are not to blame; rather Christians need to defend themselves, family members, property, and churches" (IMED93).[66] Another respondent observed, "We have given approval for self-defense for over twenty-five years in Northern Nigeria because of the recurring sense of hostility from Muslims. Should we not resort to a means of defending ourselves, families, and churches?" (GANG44).[67]

Another interviewee remarked, "I am aware that there is a Christian youth militia in our city due to severe religious violence. They react promptly in response to religious violence. In fact, some Christians have resorted to traditional [spirit] powers for occult powers. This is the medicine for self-defense" (BRUA45).[68] One participant said, "I know the formation of a group that names themselves Nehemiah Group, and they are pastors from three mainline denominations (ECWA, Baptist, and Anglican). The Nehemiah Group carries the Bible, guns, and sticks, and swears by them as the most appropriate method of taking vengeance against those who perpetrate religious violence" (AENG18).[69] Another respondent remarked, "I am from a ruling class and my grandfather was the chief custodian, warrior, and a defender of his community during wars. Since religious violence has turned to religious war, who

64. Interview Fri23Feb01.
65. Interview Fri23Feb01.
66. Interview Sun25Feb01.
67. Interview Sun30May04.
68. Interview Wed8Apr09.
69. Interview Wed15Apr09.

says we should not defend ourselves as Christians? I voted for self-defense to protect myself, family, and church" (LRUE07).[70]

However, one participant observed the fact that Muslims have not been held accountable for past violence. He said,

> I understand the Muslim agenda better, and only with a consensus believe in self-defense as a positive tool which can force the Muslims to consider the consequences of their actions in disrupting our peace in homes, churches, and now even in markets and parks everywhere in Northern Nigeria. We have taken it upon ourselves to educate other average Christians to remain on guard, as Muslim arrogance has grown, due to none of them being called to account by governmental officials for previous violence. (EUDA91)[71]

Thus, the majority of interviewees felt that use of self-defense methods was justified as a deterrent to religious violence in Northern Nigeria.

Conclusions

This research provides a comprehensive look into the lives of the respondents. In each case, the respondent's answers provided an insider's perspective of what is occurring in the events surrounding their lives in the midst of a violent environment and their responses to same. While their response may be difficult for other peoples' minds who have never experienced living in such an environment to comprehend, they remain the understood realities of the respondents. The majority of those who have become members of the ECWA have done so through what Edmund Crampton described as "fears of religious persecution and discrimination."[72] Following their conversion the overwhelming number of respondents described their early social and religious context as surrounded by discrimination, similar to what their loving founding fathers faced with both colonial officials and Muslims.

70. Interview Wed22Apr09.
71. Interview Wed29Apr09.
72. Crampton, *Christianity in Northern Nigeria*, 2nd ed., 84.

The majority of those questioned reported experiences of religious violence against themselves.

Earlier, pacifism remained a high priority among the respondents. The majority applied biblical principles in response to religious violence until when they described it to be a religious war against them. In each case, the respondents described them resorting to violent response with self-defense.

Based on these responses to the research questions, one gets a picture of the current situation of religious violence in Northern Nigeria, and the suffering that has occurred to the Christian believers there. The final chapter will look at the implications of this data, and make recommendations for further study.

CHAPTER SIX

Research Conclusions, Implications, and Recommendations for Further Research

Introduction

The main burden of this research has been to examine why some Christians in Northern Nigeria have resorted to violent means in response to religious violence despite their faith in Christ. The biblical narrative portion of the research examined the problem of violence beginning from the Old Testament on the basis of Genesis 4:8–10; 6:5–8; Psalm 10:15, 17–18; Isaiah 4:2; 9:6–7; Micah 4:3; and Joel 3:9–10. Examination of the Old Testament provides a starting point for understanding the response to religious violence.

First, the Hebrew Scriptures are not a primer on violence. Rather, with surprising fullness and diversity, they provide guidance for overcoming violence and guide readers to hinder, reject, prevent, and eliminate its causes. The Old Testament portrays violence as abnormal and pathological. Neither the original creation of Genesis 1–2 nor the eventual new creation of Revelation 21–22 has any place for violence. Second, the Old Testament literature gives hope of an ultimate end to violence, so Yahweh is said to have worked violence that belongs to the enforcement of his sovereignty (Gen 3:15;). Third, therefore, violence is not part of creation. Rather, violence is a result of the chaos, alienation, and the pride of fallen humanity (Gen 3:1–14). Fourth, the prophets continued with the announcement of the future coming of the

Prince of Peace, who will establish the new kingdom of peace (Isa 4:2, 9.6; Mic 4:3; Joel 3:9–10).

In the New Testament literature, examination reveals that, according to Paul's teaching in his epistle to the Romans, violence is replaced by creative, nonviolent alternatives (Rom 8:20–23). It is observed with the patient suffering and forgiving love already realized and experienced in God's established kingdom through Jesus Christ (Luke 24:39; John 3:16, 4:24; Heb 9:15). God's established kingdom through Jesus Christ never defined the mission of the church by conquest of land and people. Violence results from and manifests human sin and rebellion against the Creator (Gen 3; Rom 3:23, 6:23). This position comes from the teaching of Jesus Christ in Matthew 5 and other passages from the Gospels (Luke 6:20–23, 27–31). Rather, Scripture fulfilled Christ's death as foretold in the Old Testament. The sinless Son of God stands in the midst of these evils and allows violence to take place so he can redeem and free souls to the will of the Triune God to recognize all human beings as bearers of God's image in which all carnal weapons are renounced (Matt 26:50–56; 2 Cor 10:4–5).

Jesus Christ has fully exhibited God's will in a violent world (John 1:29–34, 19:30), calling Christians to peacemaking and patient suffering. Jesus Christ is the peace of Christians who has made them both one and broken hostility (Eph 2:14) and a violent ending awaits Satan and his cohorts at the end of human history (Rev 19:11–15; 20:1–10). Martin Luther's work has been extensively examined by the researcher and findings available show Martin Luther did not condone the idea of violence no matter how just it might be.

According to Luther, war is a matter of self-defense. Self-defense is a proper ground for fighting, and, therefore, all laws agree that self-defense shall go unpunished; he who kills another in self-defense is innocent in the eyes of all men. However, when Christianity was the official religion of the Roman Empire, the church saw it as duty not to only protect her own existence, but to protect others. This spurred Augustine to come up with a "just war" theory and to advocate self-defense as well as fighting for those who could not defend themselves. The researcher also examined current scholarship that contributes in providing insight that helps in responding to the problem of religious violence in our society. Current views of response to violence and suffering reveal that the Christian pilgrimage is not about the race of saints along the way to heaven, nor of the dangers and encouragement of the pilgrim, but rather a discussion of the qualifications needed to enter the gate at the end of the journey (1 Tim 2:1–5).

Findings from Field Research

The qualitative field research aspects of the study were ethnographic and phenomenological, and this study was carried out among Christians in Northern Nigeria, combined with respondents' observations. The researcher had planned to have interviews with seven participants each from thirteen states using the semi-structured interview protocol. The respondents were Christians. The researcher asked respondents to describe their social and religious experiences, conversion experiences, and the problem, causes, approaches and responses toward religious violence among the Christians.

The researcher carried out pilot interviews in Northern Nigeria and Plateau state in Jos, central Nigeria. He used English and Hausa languages among the Christians over a period of two hundred and seventy-three weeks from February to December 2001 and fifty-four more interviews with participants from June to December 2013. The central purpose of the research was to examine why some Christians in Northern Nigeria have resorted to violent means in response to religious violence. The rationale to research the problem was as a result of the bloody Muslim religious violence against Christians that has continued for decades unabated in Northern Nigeria. The research was constructed around the following four research questions: (1) What was the social and religious context in which Christians in Northern Nigeria were planted? (2) How do Christians in Northern Nigeria describe what the Christina message means to them? (3) How do Christians in Northern Nigeria describe the cause of religious violence? (4) What solutions to the problem of religious violence do Christians in Northern Nigeria propose?

The field research work has presented that Christians consider violence as a missiological menace that has battered the testimony of the church and its witness in the world. Research findings show that Christians initially responded to violence with a pacifist biblical mandate. Findings also show that during the pre-colonial days, non-Muslim groups who were not conquered by Islam lived under religious discrimination and oppression by Muslim military leaders. After the missionary societies jointly and independently resisted pro-Islamic colonial biases, the colonial authorities opened up the

Hausa Muslim areas of Northern Nigeria to mission work. Research findings established that religious violence continued after independence even more regularly. Christians took a nonviolent approach in response and followed the teaching of Christ to show their love for Christ and their violent neighbors, the Muslims. Yet Muslims continued to discriminate and attacked Christians with violence. Christians gradually got involved in an ecumenical basis through New Life for All and Christian Association of Nigeria groups in their struggles to seek religious freedom and tolerance. But Christians were not given fair hearing. Later, attention shifted during the 1960s to more aggressive struggles, culminating in violent response and constant religious war.

The basis for further resistance to Islamification was already in the impact of New Life for All and the Pentecostal movements, both of which saw large numbers of people becoming Christians, simultaneously creating militant Christians who were quite prepared to stand firm for their beliefs. Eventually, those Christians abandoned pacifism in view of their understanding that it is religious war and not persecution for their Christian faith. The research reveals that some Christians who claimed to have come to faith in Jesus Christ understand that Islam is an instrument of terror against the church requiring from them a violent response. They are antagonistic, suspicious, and seek retaliation toward their oppressors because Christians are always at the receiving end of any religious violence. There are some Christians who resort to the traditional powers of their ancestors when they are faced with violent issues in life. Their reliance on charms is perhaps due to the absence of a biblical alternative.

The research findings confirm that religious violence is escalating now in Northern Nigeria, and that the roots of the problem predate the presence of British rule with its preferential treatment of Islam over Christianity. It has also confirmed that the change from prior pacifism to Christians resorting to a violent response is due to the government's failure to protect them, in what Christians regard as a religious war. In search of a more proactive and powerful response, some Christians have accommodated the use of traditional charms, which are a compromise to their Christian faith and practice. The main question is: why do some Christians in Northern Nigeria resort to violent response to religious violence contrary to biblical practice of pacifism? How can Christianity be presented as a violent religion with a mixture of traditional beliefs in responding to violence and at the same time witness to the world (Matt 5:16)?

Research Findings and Implications

The research has unveiled some situations that have contributed to resorting to violent means to solve religious violence among Christians across Northern Nigeria. These situations are: (1) despair, desperation, uncertainty; (2) pitfalls in worldviews; (3) Pentecostal influence on young ECWA pastors in Nigeria; (4) problem of growth in numbers; (5) lack of love; (6) lack of forgiveness and reconciliation; and (7) self-defense. Other factors could have contributed to religious violence in churches, but the ones that have been pointed out are the main situations that came to the forefront in this study.

Despair, Desperation, and Uncertainty

When the participants' interviews were done, the findings established the truth that despair, desperation, and uncertainty are the major components for these Christians adopting resistance. From the beginning, when the Christians started experiencing what they perceived to be religious violence against them, they expressed their trust in God through prayer, fleeing where possible, and their leaders made appeals to the appropriate government authorities. But as more anti-Christian violence erupted, it created an atmosphere of despair, desperation, uncertainty, and a sense of threat that needed a more biblical solution. It was while in the process of exploring which would be the right response that Christians became confused, uncertain, and disunited in purpose. The events had not become stabilized enough to allow the Christians to work out better biblical alternatives and methods of response.

In their despair and uncertainty regarding which direction to take, they did not remember to ask, "Where are those who can teach us to pray for the enemy, to do good to those who hate us, to bless those who curse us, to bless and not to curse?"[1] There are lessons from Paul's teaching for Christians who are find themselves in the midst of despair and uncertainty. Paul says that hardships, if embraced by faith as a painful, but gracious gift from a loving Father (Rom 8:28–29; 35–39) draw one deeper into a transforming

1. Brown, *When God Is Silent*, 43–82.

fellowship with the Lord Jesus Christ (Phil 3:10). Such suffering produces a refined character filled with buoyant hope (Rom 5:3–5). This is why the Christian can view violence for the sake of Christ, like saving faith itself, as God's gift to his people and one that signifies their sonship (Rom 8:16–17; Phil 1:28–30). Despair of life itself should create endurance and hope to help a Christian to be totally dependent on God (2 Cor 2:9).

Pitfalls in Worldviews

Unconverted Traditional Worldview

The research findings show that some Christians have kept their traditional worldview. Paul Hiebert describes this clearly as "the three dimensions of culture." Hiebert's insights about the cultural teaching could help those Christians to re-evaluate their reception of the gospel message. The three concepts he presents about culture are (1) the "cognitive dimension," that shared body of knowledge within the community to aid communication and community life (this deals with the biblical truth of God's word); (2) the "affective dimension," which has to do with feelings of the people (this involves the good news and conversion, include feelings); and (3) the "evaluative dimension," the addressing of the right and wrong in society. Culture involves sharing the gospel in the context of underlying cultures and traditions, which is actualized in conversion.[2]

Unfortunately, contrary to the suggestions offered by Hiebert, Fuller points out that pioneers who founded the Christians in Northern Nigeria "sought to contextualize the Gospel in cultural aspects as traditional clothing and local languages. They were concerned with making the work truly indigenous, so they opposed the wearing of Western clothes and the use of English."[3] This theological perception of contextualization of traditional culture at the introduction of the gospel negates the principles of critical and comprehensive religious dimensions.[4] In order to convert the traditional worldview of any culture, Hiebert points out that there are four steps to critical contextualization. The first step is the exegesis of the culture. This engages a phenomenological approach in which the questions of right and wrong are temporarily

2. Hiebert, *Anthropological Insights*, 33–35.
3. Fuller, *Mission-Church Dynamics*, 195.
4. Pocock, *Changing Face of World Missions*, 336–39.

suspended until one is sure they understand the phenomena being considered. The second step is exegesis of Scripture and use of a hermeneutical bridge. Pastors are needed to guide the community in the study of Scriptural passages related to the question at hand. In doing this they provide a framework through which the community may translate the biblical message into all dimensions of their culture. A bridge is thus affected from the text of Scripture to their setting. The third step is a critical evaluation of a community's beliefs and cultures in the light of the new biblical understanding. The fourth step is to develop a new contextualized practice. Here, the leaders of the churches help the faith community arrange the practices and beliefs they have chosen into a ritual that expresses the Christian meaning of the event.[5]

Hiebert's method of critical contextualization needs to be appreciated by churches to engage better those members who tend to mix biblical truth with traditional life. Such critical contextualization is not based on developing a new theological system, but rather based on helping people deal theologically and practically with issues at hand. Church members also require a comprehensive understanding of Christian beliefs.[6] It involves the areas of the Christian faith to which it has to be applied.

When pastors are training people who recently came to faith from traditional backgrounds, it seems appropriate for them to look for biblical norms and models to bring to their culture, to see the ways in which God has already revealed himself in it and prepared it for the reception of the Christian faith. They are first taught that salvation is not obtained through general revelation (Rom 1:18–31). The specifics needed for salvation come through faith as a result of special revelation. Scripture alone gives it. At the same time, bridges for people to understand the gospel and its implications for church life are present in every culture, because God reveals himself to every culture long before they were converted to the new faith. The second comprehensive understanding of contextualizing in which Christians are guided is for them to come to grips with the biblical message, which shows that God is deeply

5. Hiebert, *Anthropological Insights*, 33–35.

6. See Smart, *Dimensions of the Sacred*. Smart proposed a scheme of seven dimensions that apply to all religions. Visit the web for his database resources on contextualization via http://www.mislinks.org/biblio/query.php.

concerned about human justice in every human society and for local believers to know that the kingdom of God is in their midst.

Members are to be taught to understand that traditional ways of life, religion, customs, and social values of tribal society all may be redeemed and liberated by the gospel of Christ. If such is not done, poorly taught Christians can easily revert to traditional practices and things that are not Bible-based.

Theological Pitfalls

The findings revealed that Christians inherited the fundamentalists' theological worldviews from their founding missionaries, in rejection of modernist theology. Christians usually adhered to premillennial dispensational views as against cognitive views. Biblical prophecy was a concern to them more than engagement and or reflection on the world around them. Our earlier findings have already established that when the missionaries brought the gospel, they aimed at only converting individuals. They failed to convert the cultures from which these individuals came. The founding missionaries' theological worldviews again prevented them from bringing to light the conversion viewpoints of the decision-making process that Tippet proposes. There are four possibilities open to gospel hearers: the first is conversion, simply rejecting the old and accepting the new; the second is rejection, retaining the old and rejecting the new; the third is secularism, rejecting the old and rejecting the new; and then the fourth is syncretism, retaining the old and accepting the new.[7] The context of Tippet's analysis is relevant to Christians, in that some of them might have accepted Christ, but it became hard for them to relinquish the old traditional beliefs by invoking charms to respond to violence because of their incomprehensive theological beliefs.

The implication for Christians in Northern Nigeria is that they became Christians without the benefit of a theology with which to confront crises. That also means most of them are ignorant regarding others, and hence there is shallow knowledge of the complete biblical view of life in the world in which they live. The rise of Pentecostalism demonstrates the vacuum that this theological deficiency created.

---

7. Van Rheenen, *Contextualization and Syncretism*, 94–95.

Pentecostal Influence on Young ECWA Pastors in Nigeria

"Evangelical Church Winning All (ECWA) has over 10 million members in Nigeria and some 10,000 pastors of local churches in Nigeria."[8] A respondent remarked that "there is no doubt that Pentecostalism has penetrated and influenced ECWA Pastors positively and negatively especially on certain areas of doctrinal matters such as pneumatology, faith gospel deliverance, and healing." This respondent further mentioned that "The entrance of the gospel to village life as presented by the pioneering missions to Africa did not enable the young people to understand doctrinal standards that would help them to face situations." Johnstone and Mandryk write, "Younger people have been particularly influenced in churches by Pentecostalism. This is not only in relation to worship styles or charismatic perception to social issues, public speaking in tongues, prosperity Gospel, miraculous healing and deliverance from demonic powers."[9] For example in the Nigerian context, popular level of Pentecostal styles of music, prayer and liturgy and Pentecostal worship often appeals to young people in the church. With regards to worship, the expression of Pentecostal way of worship practice has influenced a lot of ECWA pastors to emphasis volume in their worship services. They force their congregations to express their emotions and energy through singing and clapping for several minutes in a standing position. By contrast, Keener argues that "worship does not involves merely enjoying the rhythm of a song, experiencing an emotional feeling, or comprehending a liturgy, helpful as any of these may sometimes be for inviting our attention to God."[10] Keener ends by saying, "God wants us to worship him in sincere desire for his honor. We should ask him and trust him to turn our hearts toward him."[11]

But in its original setting in the United States of America Pentecostalism had sound biblical intentions. In order to understand this, it is necessary to examine the original and historical setting of the movement. What may a

8. Baba (then ECWA President, at SIM's 125 anniversary celebration), as reported in *Today's Challenge*, vol 15.1 January 2019, Challenge Press, Jos, Nigeria, 17 and quoted in Dadang, "125 Years of Serving in Mission (SIM)", 64.

9. Johnstone and Mandryk, *Operation World*, 489.

10. Keener, *Gift Giver: Holy Spirit for Today* (Grand Rapids, Michigan: Baker Acedimic,2001),32.

11. Keener, 33.

researcher say were the historical factors leading to the worldwide expansion of Pentecostalism?

Burgess and Vander Maas noted that "Historians often trace the origins of Pentecostalism in the United States to a revival that began on Jan. 1901, at Charles F. Parham's Bethel Bible School in Topeka, Kansas."[12] Burgess and Mass reiterate that, "with the identification of speaking tongues as the evidence of baptism in the Holy Spirit, Parham and his students made a vital theological connection that has remained essential to much of classical Pentecostalism."[13] While the immediate impact of this event was limited, Parham's ministry gained more acceptance several years later in a revival conducted outside Houston, Texas.[14] "From there William J. Seymour, an [African] Holiness preacher who had become convinced of the truth of Parham's teaching on spirit baptism traveled to Los Angeles, California, to preach the new message."[15] This suggests that William Joseph Seymour was an important figure in the spread of Pentecostalism. Hollenweger explains that Seymour (1870–1922) was born to the son of a former slave from Centerville, Louisiana. He taught himself to read and write and was for a time a student in Charles Fox Parham's Bible school in Topeka, Kansas.[16] Hollenweger, however notes that Parham (1873–1929), often described as a pioneer of Pentecostalism, was also a sympathizer of the Ku Klux Klan – he therefore excluded Seymour from his Bible classes. He adds that, "Seymour accepted Parham's doctrine of the baptism of the Spirit and began to teach it in a Holiness church in Los Angeles."[17]

Burgess and Mass explained that the ensuing revival at the Azusa Street mission (1906–1909) represented an anomaly on the America religious scene, such that racial barriers were broken; African, Whites, and Hispanics worshipped together. Men and women shared leadership responsibilities. The barrier between clergy and laity vanished. The participants believed that the

12. Burgess and Mass, *International Dictionary*, xviii.
13. Burgess and Mass, xviii.
14. Burgess and Mass, xviii.
15. Burgess and Mass, xviii.
16. Hollenweger, *Pentecostalism*, 19.
17. Hollenweger, 19.

endowment with spiritual power for ministry was intended to be received by all.[18] Furthermore, according to Burgess and Mass,

> the gifts of the Holy Spirit (1 Cor. 12) understood by most denominations as having ceased at the end of the first century, had been restored . . . From Los Angeles, news of the outpouring of the Holy Spirit spread across the nation and around the world by word of mouth and the printed page. Before long, Pentecostals revival could be found in Canada, England, Scandinavian, Germany, India, Africa and South America.[19]

Burgess and Maas, further comment that "theological issues soon began to divide the movement concerning the nature of sanctification, the gift of tongues, and the trinity generated tensions that remained."[20] The racial harmony of Azusa Street waned within few mouths, and as a result Pentecostalism remains racially divided with very limited progress toward reconciliation.[21] Pentecostalism's journey to Africa had deep roots in South Africa. Hollenweger notes that, "In South Africa, Pentecostalism started as an integrated church and developed – as in the USA – into a segregated church."[22] He further comments that the early missionaries to South Africa, had both worshipped in Seymour's church and were already acquainted with the non-racial commitment and practice of Seymour at the Azusa street mission.[23]

Wacker offers a theological and historical meaning of the Pentecostal experience as follows. (1) Early Pentecostals believed they lived in a world constantly visited by supernatural activity to the extent that even the most mundane events were perceived as divine intervention, judgment, or blessings. (2) They expected that God would signal the second coming of Christ at any time. (3) Pentecostals preached ascetic doctrine, stressing the importance of perfection, strict moral ethics, and biblical inerrancy. (4) They exhorted believers to shun all unnecessary material and carnal pleasures. (5) Finally,

18. Burgess and Mass, *International Dictionary*, xviii.
19. Burgess and Mass, xviii.
20. Burgess and Mass, xviii.
21. Burgess and Mass, xviii.
22. Hollenweger, *Pentecostalism*, 41.
23. Hollenweger, 19.

Pentecostal assumptions were viewed in light of their eschatological hopes.[24] Pentecostal doctrines stress the experience of the filling of the Holy Spirit. This is deeply rooted in the origins, development and history of Pentecostalism. Having explained the origin and development of Pentecostalism, it is important to understand the journey and impact on Christians in Africa.

Kalu, notes that "in contemporary Christianity, Pentecostalism has become a major force constituting about a quarter of the world's two billion Christians, and the number of Pentecostals has grown by stressing an intimate and joyous relationship with God, adapting to local cultures, especially groups that have strong beliefs in the spirit world and by focusing on healing, prophecy and God's direct intervention in the material well-being of his people."[25] The coming of Pentecostalism in Nigeria encouraged ecumenical union with other churches, but the context of unity in shared belief and practice was unfortunately not sustained. Kalu opines that "Pentecostal existence should be set within a larger picture that shows that ministerial formation continues to be a problem for all the churches in Africa because the rapid growth calls to question the viability of inherited patterns and walled institutions."[26] Kalu, explained "Now, the number of believers, types of Pentecostalism, forms of Christian worship, high level of competition, conflicting theologies, rivalry and jealous demarcation of turf among groups of believers complicate the problem."[27] The habit of pastors not receiving sound biblical teaching means that pastors can be carried away in ministry by winds of doctrine that encourage a nominal life that fails to deal with the crises of daily Christian living. Christians need to learn from this teaching of Luther:

> Two things to be important for everyday Christian existence are knowledge of sin and forgiveness, and trusting God as the one who rules the world in small and in great. They are to be soldiers of Christ who are Biblically nourished. They are to be soldiers of Christ who understand that the power struggles are already theirs and have been completed in the power of the

24. Wacker, *Heaven Below*, 380.

25. Kalu, *African Pentecostalism: An Introduction* (Oxford, New York: Oxford University Press, 2008),xiv.

26. Kalu,126.

27. Kalu,127.

finished work of Christ on the cross when Jesus said, "It is finished" (John 19:30).[28]

Pastors have the obligation to teach that the reason for church membership is to engage believers in real Christian discipleship and the growth of Christ's body. The nominal Christian life is a problem among Christians because of the emphasis on growth in numbers rather than spiritual maturity and the equipping of their members for spiritual service.

Although some members in ECWA were attracted to Pentecostal way of preaching prosperity gospel, some theologically trained did not favor prosperity teaching. Speaking on the challenge of the prosperity gospel for Christians, Okwori writes that "the prosperity Gospel could not have originally been conceived in Africa."[29]

Pentecostalism proclaims a transformational gospel replacing the old ways of patriarchal and animistic domination with divine power available through the individual person and blood of Jesus and the work of the Holy Spirit. Lives of individuals and communities are transformed, and God's kingdom is extended. Its doctrinal beliefs include speaking in tongues, prosperity, extension of the efficacy of the blood of Jesus Christ from atonement to every aspect of life, and a literal interpretation of the word of God. Communities tend to turn their ears to the sound of the gospel and in so doing previously accepted customs and beliefs are exposed. This transformation and exposure provokes vigorous reactions from those committed the old ways such as traditional rulers or those in politics. Traditionally, there is no clear demarcation between secular politics and religion. The one informs the other, so the spiritual is used in empowering the secular and it in turn rewards the secular's allegiance. Whether through traditional beliefs, Islam, or Christianity, religion is the context within which things operate. Pentecostals share this understanding of the religious basis to secular power. Pentecostals teach that instead of relying on the old ways, which they believe have resulted in the state's failure, they tend to offer a new way. In the Pentecostal view, the new way is actualized by transforming individuals, addressing the social problems and moral failings of the state, asserting the rule of the saints, and building new communities. Kalu affirms "A significant dimension of Pentecostalism

28. Barth, *Theology of Martin Luther*, 368.

29. Okwori, *Godliness for Gain*, 5–7.

evangelism is the proliferation of missionary strategies among Pentecostals."[30] Kalu notes that "Pentecostals affirm that when the Holy Spirit calls and sends, He will supply the material needs to fulfill the mission."[31] Kalu concludes, "but churches do not sit down and wait for the manna; rather they engage in a number of strategies to raise funds."[32]

Problem of Growth in Numbers

The researcher in one of his findings confirmed that the pioneers who planted congregations across Nigeria seemed to have had foresight. Their missionary practice in starting a church began by acquiring land and building in the location in which they wished to organize a congregation. They provided housing for their missionaries. However, a minor oversight was how the local communities were not involved with the process. The work was progressive. They opened three new mission stations, at Pategi in 1901, Miango in 1912, and in Jos in 1926. They built new mission hospitals with funds they independently raised from the overseas churches from which they came. They also handled all the financial transactions themselves. Another oversight was how they quickly handed over the churches and hurriedly introduced what many missiologists refer to as the self-governing, self-supporting, and self-propagating philosophy without giving enough time to discipleship to bring Christians to maturity. When they handed over the work to the indigenous Christians, they initially encountered challenges. First, since the nationals were not involved in the projects, they had inadequate funds to maintain the structures. Second, they were not taught how to raise funds for projects so they did not know how to write for grants. Third, they could not provide adequate upkeep for the hospitals and clinics that SIM built. The researcher wishes that the missionaries had taken the advice of Schulz that "no longer should planting efforts focus on creating replicas of the church body back home or that entity which sponsors the projects."[33]

Christians did not have the opportunity to be equipped by their planters (Eph 4:11–13). This contributed to some living nominal Christian lives,

30. Kalu, *African Pentecostalism: An Introduction*,133.

31. Kalu, *African Pentecostalism: An Introduction*,141.

32. Kalu,141.

33. Schulz, *Mission from the Cross*, 207.

seeming outside the kingdom of Christ. Nominalism can lead to exerting deadening unscriptural views and inadequate preparation of seekers for baptism.

Nominal Christian Life

A participant said,

> I know that in a given church only 40 percent less might be faithful believers and active members who believe and practice the Bible, and this gives room for nominal Christian living. In Jos, there are those who go to churches that consult mediums. If they are doing this in churches where one would expect that people are born again, then it means Christians feel free to do anything, including buying charms. (PAAM31)

Because of inadequate Bible teaching, nominal Christians are likely to respond to violence in ways different from genuine believers in Christ. The situation is difficult to figure out because spiritual growth is beyond human measurement. In the researcher's over thirty years of leadership experience, when the need arose to interview someone for placement in pastoral and or administrative positions, it was always one the most difficult moments because few could explain their Christian faith. In the researcher's congregation, only 30 percent of church members stay for communion at the end of Sunday morning worship services (out of a regular average of 75 percent attending members). Luther "found two things to be important for everyday Christian existence, knowledge of sin and forgiveness, and trusting God as the one who rules the world in small things and in great."[34] Christians are required to apply Luther's principle. They are to be soldiers of Christ who are biblically nourished. They are to be soldiers of Christ who understand that the power struggles they face are already won by the victory of the finished work of Christ on the cross when Jesus said, "It is finished" (John 19:30). Pastors have an obligation to teach their members that the reason for church membership is true Christian discipleship and the growth and edification of the body of Christ. Nominal life is a problem among Christians because of

34. Barth, *Theology of Martin Luther*, 368.

the emphasis on numerical growth rather than nurturing and equipping the members for stewardship (Acts 2:42–47).

Lack of Preparing Those Who Seek Baptism

An understanding of baptism begins from Paul's teaching that members of churches in the New Testament consisted of baptized believers who professed Jesus as lord and savior. But it seems as if some pastors do not adequately and regularly teach the importance of baptism. Witherington reminds pastors that Acts provides evidence that the early church regularly practiced those ordinances.[35] It should be a concern in churches that pastors leave to lay people the task of preparing new converts for baptism. Pastors and the Christian education departments of churches should know that equipping new converts prepares them for spiritual battle. It prepares them to stand firm in the midst of violence and other life crises. Such an important teaching should not be left to be handled by non-ordained laity with no theological background. The researcher can argue from Paul's teaching that it was not his goal to merely win converts, but to plant churches that remain strong (Rom 16:5; 1 Cor 16:19; Col 4: 15; Phlm 1:2). If church pastors want to have church members to be baptized believers who profess Jesus as lord and savior, they should consider the importance of teaching the converts themselves. If they take that assignment seriously, those seeking baptism will be prepared in such a biblical manner that they see themselves as part of the members of Christ's universal church who are truly regenerate (Phil 4:3; 1 Tim 2:19). If churches do what they can to ensure that converts are adequately taught so that they become members who are genuinely rooted in Christ's love, they will be enabled to discern why they suffer and live by the truth of the gospel, instead of perceiving a violent response to life crises as a virtue.

Paul's teaching portrays the church as the gathered people of God who put their trust in the risen Christ (1 Cor 11:23–26, 15:1–33). The church is to have a clear doctrinal stand. Evangelism is not to be interpreted in a narrow sense of "saving souls," but in a wider and practical sense of serving the world that God so loved and gave his only son, Jesus, to serve (John 3:16).

35. Witherington, *Acts of the Apostles.*

Lack of Love

The research findings show that the problem of Christians in Northern Nigeria is usually whether to respond to violence with violence or with love. This is because the theology of pacifism seems not to be put into practice as it was previously. Kalu explains the reason behind this development that a certain theology among the Christians could be dubbed the "third slap doctrine" sustained the new determination to avenge violent attacks."[36] Kalu further explains "the argued that when the Bible encouraged them to turn their cheek, it provided for only two slaps. After a second slap, the Bible is silent, and therefore, one could avenge oneself on the basis of that silence."[37] Agang concludes, "pacifism is against all forms of violence. It draws our attention to the fact that violence is not only an enemy without, but also within persons. We may not have to go into a physical war. Yet, we must fight the spiritual battle."[38] Agang, further notes, "in teaching about turning the other cheek, Jesus was essentially stating the obvious to help them understand a not-so-obvious principle of life in a violent context."[39] Agang reiterates "He wanted them to know that they could non-violently force their oppressors to recognize their human dignity."[40]

The biblical context of being nonviolent is based on, "Love the Lord your God with all your heart and with all your soul and with your entire mind" (Matt 22:37–40). and "Love your neighbor as yourself" (Mark 12:29–31). The church is called to be witnesses to truth, justice, and righteousness in personal and public conduct (Matt 5:13–16). Christians are distinct in the world (John 17:16; Rom 12:2; 2 Cor 6:7), because they endeavor to transform the world. Elford writes, "This is why Christians are enjoined to be active makers in the present and are not permitted to believe peace will only occur in some messianic future."[41] Augsburger states, "Theologically, God in grace is creating people, a people known as members of the kingdom of God. Christological,

36. Kalu, *African Pentecostalism: An Introduction*,242.

37. Kalu,242.

38. Agang, Sunday Bobai, *When Evil Strikes: Faith and the Politics of Human Hostility* (Eugene, Oregon: PICKWICK Publications,2016),53.

39. Agang, *No More Cheeks to turn* (Carlisle, Cumbria: Hippo Books, and imprint of ACTS, Langham Publishers, 2017),57.

40. Agang, 58.

41. Gill, *Cambridge Companion*, 171.

the full revelation of God is Jesus Christ in what He said, did, and was."[42] Kunhiyop makes the case that,

> We have no more cheeks to turn. Christ was not advocating pacifism, but a constructive, non-violent resistance compatible with self-defense. Scriptures clearly forbid taking vengeance whether through violence or civil courts. Turning the other cheek is not a passive submission, but an active assertion of one's dignity and value as a human being.[43]

Volf, a Croatian theologian, offers four principles in understanding the importance of the cross in the context of violence. (1) The cross breaks the cycle of violence when Christ took on the aggression of his persecutors by absorbing it. He refused to be conformed to his enemies' violent image; (2) the cross lays bare the mechanism of scapegoating, and Jesus was deliberately chosen as the scapegoat; (3) the cross is part of Jesus's struggle for God's truth and justice ("Active opposition to the kingdom of Satan, the kingdom of deception and oppression, is therefore inseparable from the proclamation of the kingdom of God. It is this opposition that brought Jesus to the cross; and it is this opposition that gave meaning to His nonviolence"); and (4) the cross is a divine embrace of the deceitful and the unjust; in Christ, God did not ignore sin, but he told the truth about sin, and atoned for it ("The cross of Christ should teach us that the only alternative to violence is self-giving love; willingness to embrace the other in the knowledge that truth and justice have been and will be, upheld by God.").[44]

Allen points out that "the most distinctive mark of Christianity is not a set of religious ideals or ethical principles, but it is to the life-giving Gospel of Christ crucified and risen, a commitment-proven willingness to suffer for its pure proclamation."[45] The apostle Paul is an example in the following ways. (1) His sufferings were endured for the edification of the church, the body of Christ; (2) the suffering of the apostle, and, by extension that of the churches, certifies their identification with Jesus, the suffering servant; (3) the

42. Clouse, *War*, 82.
43. Kunhiyop, *African Christian Ethics*, 133, 151, 161–62.
44. Volf, *Exclusion and Embrace*, 290–95.
45. Allen, *Paul's Missionary Methods*, 96–100.

apostle's hardships are marks of authenticity on as a true servant of Christ. His physical sufferings brand him as one who belongs to Jesus (Gal 6:17).

The gospel speaks to all aspects of life and meets the yearnings of the body, mind, and spirit. It engages stewardship in God's world, past, present, and future. Christians and pastors in Northern Nigeria are to teach members that Paul's theology of suffering is not a self-deprecating delight for its own sake. Rather, harsh realities such as physical ailments, aggressive opponents, malicious verbal attacks, and even physical assaults crush every form of self-reliance so that God's triumphant power can flow (2 Cor 12:7–10).

The absence of a clear understanding of the theology of the cross may have led to nominal Christian life among some Christians in Northern Nigeria.

Lack of Forgiveness and Reconciliation

The researcher observed from findings that there were only five out of eighty-four participants that indicated any interest in forgiving their enemies. It indicates that 95 percent of those interviewed simply gave up the idea of forgiveness, much less reconciling with their enemies. It appears that they see little relevance in forgiving their enemies, and they would prefer to continue in the culture of revenge. Some Christians appear to miss out on their daily living and interaction due to the resultant bitterness caused by violence. They tend not to understand that forgiveness is the power of God's compassionate love in Jesus that trumps all that is thrown at them in life. In the New Testament, Jesus speaks of forgiveness often. He preaches it in the Sermon on the Mount. One of Jesus's popular parables in Luke 15:11–31 should teach Christians in Northern Nigeria that forgiveness is a higher calling in approaching and healing hurts. Inrig says, "Where there is forgiveness of sins, there is life and blessedness."[46] Forgiveness is Christ himself lifting the burden of the assailant. Forgiveness dilutes the power of the perpetrator to nothing. Although forgiveness is not reconciliation, a nonviolent heart desires reconciliation.

Miller writes, "Practicing non-violence enables Christians to keep the door open to reconciliation and to keep the issues in focus."[47] Forgiveness is not reconciliation. Reconciliation takes place when everyone is convinced that their grievances have been resolved and when they know justice was been

46. Inrig, *Forgiveness*, 48.

47. Miller, *Nonviolent*, 168.

served. There is no reconciliation without achieving justice. Forgiveness and reconciliation are not possible without implementing the command of Jesus to love one's enemies and to forgive them. Brothers and sisters in the church in Northern Nigeria are called to apply only love of enemies and determination not to use force to win conflicts. Hatred and wars have never restored peace.

Kober guides Christians by noting that "reconciliation is not a planned program, but a life-style. Reconciliation through confession and forgiveness can be experienced in specific events, but our Lord never intended His ministry be only reserved for occasions."[48] Miller counsels, "Practicing nonviolence enables the Christians to keep the door open to reconciliation, and to keep the issues in focus."[49] The church has been called to the ministry of healing and reconciliation. However, it seems when one becomes the victim of aggression, self-defense is permitted for Christians. Self-defense has been adopted not only by Christians, but by Nigerian Christians in general. Nonetheless, the church is called to a ministry of healing and reconciliation.

Adopting Self-Defense

Further research findings show that self-defense has been adopted among Christians in Northern Nigeria. Self-defense has a long tradition not only among Christians; Nigerian Christians in general feel that when the government is not able to maintain of law and order, it is appropriate to adopt self-defense. Christians argue that when one is outside the protection of armed authority, possession of arms for protection of family and the weak is appropriate. Kunhiyop maintains that "this is the clearest position on self-defense. Self-defense is proper. A position of nonviolent in dealing with oppression and injustice does not contradict a position of self-defense or defense of family, or even one's church."[50]

Luther concludes that a Christian lives not in himself, but in Christ and his neighbor. Otherwise, he is not a Christian. Christians therefore, do not fight as individuals or for their own benefits, but as obedient servants of the authorities under whom they live. Luther, says, "Whoever starts a war is in

48. Kober, *Confessions and Forgiveness*, 170.

49. Miller, *Nonviolent*, 168.

50. Kunhiyop, *Africa Christian Ethics*, 164.

the wrong."[51] War for the Christian believer needs be a matter of self-defense. "Self-defense is a proper ground for fighting and, therefore, all laws agree that self-defense shall go unpunished, and he who kills another in self-defense is innocent in the eyes of all men."[52] According to Luther, "The reason for self-defense and just war is simply that every lord and prince is bound to protect his people and preserve the peace for them. That is his office; that is why he has the sword (Romans 13:[14])."[53]

Christians are reminded that the position of nonviolence is on the basis of Christ's teaching Matthew 22:37–40, "Love the Lord your God will all your heart, and with all your soul and with your entire mind, and love your neighbor as yourself; all the law and the prophets stand on these two commandments" (see also Mark 12:29–31). The church is a witness to truth, justice, and righteousness in its personal and public conduct. The church is called to be salt and light of the world (Matt 5:13–16). The implication for Christians is to engage the world by being light and salt in their community (Rom 12:2; 1 Cor 6:7; Col 3:1–5).

Missiological Contribution of the Response to Violence

The researcher has gained insight from responses to the question, what is a proper biblical theology of suffering, persecution, and response to religious violence? Violence, sufferings, persecution, and death did not originate in the twenty-first century, as examined in this research. Not only are violence, suffering, persecution, and death not new, they have not yet ceased. As Christians, we look to the final consummation of the kingdom as the ultimate remedy and end to the world's problems. Political and humanitarian efforts may heal certain symptoms of violence, but they cannot cure the underlying disease of sin. Eitel rightly notes, "It is thus easy for a Christian to have compassion for people and their eternal destinies to embrace D. L. Moody's image of seeking to pull into the heavenly lifeboat as many souls

51. Luther, *Luther's Works*, vol. 45, 118.

52. Luther, 120.

53. Luther, 122.

as possible [including the likely vessel of Muslims violence] away from the sinking ship of this world."[54]

The researcher is not saying the biblical theology of suffering, persecution, and response to religious violence is final. There could be more missiological contributions in addition to what the researcher is proposing in response to religious violence. There are four distinctive Christian missiological concerns about suffering and violence in regard to Muslim violence than can be embraced across Christian response to religious violence.

The first missiological principle is our inherent Christian trait that portrays Christians belonging to the heavenly kingdom that cuts across all boundaries whose citizenship is in heaven (Phil 3:20). As those who have the identity of Christ in us, we suffer and rejoice together and his identity compels us to live in peace and comfort in violent situations (Rom 12:15).

The second missiological principle is the divine calling Christians have to be salt and light to the world (Matt 5:16). As Christians, Jesus Christ has defined our agenda, and because we love him, we are constrained to embrace as well the mandate he has given the church. Evangelism and witness to Jesus Christ is one distinctive Christian way of dealing with violence and suffering connected with Muslim-Christian violence in Northern Nigeria or elsewhere in Africa.

The third missiological principle in which all Christians in Northern Nigeria agree in responding to Muslim violence and Christian suffering is that the Triune God reigns over the entire world. Everything that exists and happens in this world is under God's sovereignty. Christians can thus approach violence, sufferings, persecution, and death with confidence that our heavenly ruler is aware, concerned, and involved (John 19:16).

The fourth missiological principle is a holistic approach to ministry that is embodied in social concerns, emotional concerns, physical concerns, and spiritual concerns. The most effective response to religious violence is to teach theological truths in the process of discipleship and maturing relationships (Matt 28:19, 20). Spiritual concepts should be developed within the framework of the questions and the concerns of daily life. Discipleship in this context focuses on helping people know God in the midst of difficult

54. Eitel, *Missions in Contexts of Violence*, 20.

circumstances. A theology of the cross and suffering is addressed through biblical concepts of discipleship.

Those who are involved in theological education can take the lead by taking steps to promote an atmosphere of training of seminary students how to build relationships with people of other religions without compromising biblical standards. It will lead the pastors in training to break barriers that are hindrances and build relationships that lead to peace.

Recommendations for Further Research

The Problem of Religious Violence in Northern Nigeria

The research work has provided a foundation for further careful research with regards to the problem of responding to violence among Christians in Northern Nigeria and in Africa. Of course, no one can claim that this work has unearthed all solutions to the problem of religious violence among Christians in Northern Nigeria. Some patterns of Christians' responses to the challenges of resurgent violence, cloudy theological worldviews, and the desire to resort to a violent response to religious violence rather than turning to the God of love have not been adequately addressed in this research work. This researcher emphasizes that research is not to be considered complete, but rather a foundation block for theologians in Northern Nigeria to continue research in the area of Christian response to religious violence among Christians in Northern Nigeria, a Christian ethical and theological topic that seems so complex that little attention is given to it. It seems that no field research work has been done in Northern Nigeria in the area of Christian response to religious violence among Christians. The fear of Christians suffering appears to be the first burden among Christians in Northern Nigeria. It appears their understanding of God's kingdom is not sufficient for them to come to terms with the fact that the gospel is not that they can save themselves from danger, but rather that God loves them and that with his divine help, they can love others and die for their love in Christ.

Research on the theology of the cross and suffering would be a good area that would help Christians in Northern Nigeria to have a better focus on responding not only to Islamic provocation that often results in religious violence, but other social crises of life. Articulating an adequate theology of suffering will help the church in working out biblical ways in which members should respond to the regular forms of religious violence that occur.

Response to Pentecostal Theological Teaching on Suffering

Maintaining a theological standard is a subject of research for Christians. Theologians need to respond to Pentecostal teaching. There is a limited response to the pressures of many of the youth that are attracted by the lively worship, promise of answers for their social and economic needs, and the miraculous. While there is need for research on the biblical way to conduct contemporary worship, there is also the need to research the preferential treatment of the poor in the church of Northern Nigeria. This research will really help in determining whether poverty and other social problems drive Christian youth to Pentecostalism and whether economic problems push them to participate in a violent response to religious violence.

Research on Forgiveness and Reconciliation in the Context of Religious Violence

Another kind of research to be done in the future could include the areas of forgiveness and reconciliation. The research findings presented that there has been a long period of hurts, grieves, bitterness among Christians toward their neighbors, the Muslims. The research on forgiveness and reconciliation would give Christians' ways to keep their doors open to the search for justice, to love, and to forgiveness. Should the research succeed, nonviolent responses would allow room for dialogue and reconciliation when feelings subside. Reconciliation happens when everyone feels their grievances have been resolved and justice has been served. All of these take place when the biblical teaching to love and forgive your enemies has been implemented. Another area of research might be in the area of how to build relationships with people of other religions without compromising biblical standards. This research, if conducted, can lead to breaking down barriers and building relationships that lead to peace.

Research on Proper Responses to Nominal Christians

The matter of the searching for power through invoking the spirits of ancestors to have charms in response to religious violence was a complex subject among participants. Nominal Christianity is widespread among Christians in

Nigeria. Whether such is an adequate explanation for reliance on the power of charms gives room for further research on the subject. One would think that reliance on the power of charms has to do more with deficiency in biblical teaching of the churches or a lack of proper understanding of *missio Dei*. If Christians are not nourished in the word, they may fall into an anemic spiritual life. While there is the need for adequate teaching and proper attention to biblical doctrine and good hermeneutics and homiletics workshops, a phenomenological study on why some Christians use charms for power in response to religious violence needs to be pursued.

Impact of Missiology and *Missio Dei* on Response to Religious Violence

The research findings revealed that the Danish Lutheran missionaries prepared their converts to face challenges in society immediately. Independence was gained. Since then, the Lutheran churches in Northern Nigeria appear to have developed a comprehensive alternative approach for responding to religious violence. A Bible-believing missiologist from Northern Nigeria needs to undertake research among the Lutheran churches in Northern Nigeria and how they respond to violence differently from conservative Christians. The researcher shares a common Christian faith. However, there is need for further research on eschatology and missiology as it impacts areas touched by religious violence. The researcher wishes to reiterate his theological conviction that true *missio Dei* acknowledges that the distance between God and humanity is already bridged in Christ by the Holy Spirit and through his active church, and not that mission bridges the gap between God and humanity (John 3:17; 5:30; 11:42; 14:26; 16:7; 17:18). The incarnation of God in Jesus Christ is the union of a divine and human nature in one person (John 1.1–4, 14; 10:30). Jesus needed to possess both the divine and human natures in order to redeem humanity (John 1:29–34). Divine power was necessary in order to affect the redemption, and Christ's humanity was necessary in order for the redemption to be accomplished in it (Col 1:13–14, 19–20). The peak is the cross, death, and his resurrection (John 19:30, 11:25; 1 Pet 1:3). The Logos, the second person of the Trinity who became incarnate in Jesus Christ, is never without the human nature. Christ's relationship of potency was an entirely voluntary act of the most extreme self-renunciation imaginable (Phil 2:6–7). The Trinitarian concept is that salvation consists in its fullness of acts by God the Father sending forth the Son and the Father and Son sending the Holy Spirit. Hence, the relationship of the divine and human natures in the person of Christ remains united (John 1:1–5, 14, 10:30). In the economy of *missio Dei*, God the Father sends the Son, the Father and the Son send the Holy Spirit, and the Triune God sends the church.

Therefore, missiology is a multidisciplinary academic study that critically reflects on the mission of the church as the instrument of the salvific activity of the Triune God. It integrates various disciplines; for example, biblical, historical, systematic, and ecclesiastical theology, mission, history, and empirical studies such as linguistics and translations, statistic, cultural anthropology, psychology, education, and the studies of other religions that desire to contribute positively and constructively toward the church's faithful stewardship of the *missio Dei* (Rev 22:13, 14). Further research on the role of responding to religious violence as it relates to the subject of missiology is needed.

Epilogue

The epilogue of this dissertation has two components. The first is to help Christians, pastors, missionaries, and leaders who are in the Lord's vineyard in Northern Nigeria to understand the reason for their existence in the world, their humanity, and their behaviors as they endure sufferings and cope with the realities and fragility of life. The second is that it will inculcate biblical awareness not only in Christians, but in their theologians, pastors, and leaders in Northern Nigeria or elsewhere for Christians to serve God and live as a witness to the world. This will help in communicating and preaching the gospel message to Northern Nigerian people in such a way that speaks to their contemporary social and spiritual needs so that it will answer the questions of life they are asking. God requires total love and commitment from his children of light toward their neighbors who are still in the dark. When they reach the understanding that violent living is counterproductive and self-defeating to existence, it will help them approach better and respond appropriately to religious violence. It will further help them to understand that resorting to a violent life does not solve any conflict, but rather it suppresses human existence, and prevents peace and church growth. So if Christians are serious in putting to practice the teaching of Jesus to love their neighbors and they are committed to God, they will shine for Christ without distraction (Phil 2:16). They will experience forgiveness and reconciliation leading to healing and praying constantly for their enemies to have respect for human life and dignity now and forever.

The researcher is exhorting Christians in Northern Nigeria to recognize Jesus as Lord and trust him and always be prepared to give an answer for the reason of their hope with gentleness as part of their suffering for Christ in their context of living in a violent environment (1 Pet 3:15). Nevertheless, the researcher maintains that in a situation where the enemy has targeted Christian families and churches for war and destruction, it is necessary and appropriate for a person to take the sword and defend oneself, family, and property. Failing to do so is considered an unwise decision, irrational for a person who lives in a violent environment in which governments fail in their responsibility to protect the lives and property of citizens in a given nation such as Nigeria.

APPENDIX ONE

Interview Protocol

The interview protocol questions were centered around the social and religious context; loyalties and experiences before conversion; conversion experience, and cause(s); personal impact of religious violence on their lives and churches; relating biblical principles to enemies and what they considered to be solutions to religious violence.

I. **Life – Social and Religious Context**
   A. Can you explain to me a bit about your previous Christian background?
   B. Briefly tell me about your previous religious beliefs before you came to the Christian faith.

The answers to these protocol questions by respondents helped the researcher ascertain their previous religious foundation and beliefs were prior to Christianity. It also helped in discerning whether their religious world views were solidly established.

II. **What Salvation Means to Them**
   A. Can you tell me how your loyalty was before you became a Christian and a member in your church?
   B. Tell me how you understand salvation and the importance of baptism.
   C. Could please describe clearly to me the location of your conversion when did your conversion happen and how you became a Christian? Please, explain to me about your experience where were you, church, home, or village.

The protocol questions helped the researcher to know from respondents their Christian commitments and their membership in the church and the value of the sacraments that members of Christ's body are required to partake in. This was important and helpful to the researcher in finding out how their conversion took place and to help classify the participants properly in this research.

III. Understanding the Cause(s) of Religious Violence

A. Can you share with me what is your cardinal understanding of what seem to be the cause(s) of religious violence?

B. Tell me what you consider to be reason for Muslim violence against Christians.

C. Describe what impact has religious violence has on your Christian practice.

D. Please tell me how you personally experienced religious violence.

E. What do you perceive is happening with your church?

F. Explain to me in what ways has religious violence has impact on your church.

These protocol questions sought to find out what impact does religious violence cause on personal lives of participants and how has it affected their churches. It was aimed at finding out the level and extent to which religious violence destroy or affect their emotions, caused lives, and church property, and if so, how they reacted and described those experiences.

IV. Finding Solutions to Religious Violence

A. Please, tell me how do you relate Bible teaching in context of religious violence?

B. How do you see yourself in relationship with those the Bible ask you to love them?

C. Describe to me your personal experience on how you are to love someone who comes to kill you in the name of their religion?

D. Tell me what scriptural passage do you have in mind that you use in solving religious violence?

E. As a Christian, describe to me what you consider to be the solution(s) you propose in response to the challenges Muslim violence against Christianity in Northern Nigeria.

F. Describe to me the possible step(s) you can take to reconcile with someone who violates you, a family member, or your relative.

These sets of protocol questions were to help toward determining what participants' thoughts would be concerning their biblical understanding and responses toward violence against them given their exposure to unending Muslim violence against them, their families, churches, and their property. It was also helpful for the researcher to understand what solutions they provide as a means in response to end religious violence against them.

APPENDIX TWO

The Transmittal Letter

Dear Sir or Madam,

I am happy that you have agreed to meet with me for an interview. Thank you for your kindness and love. My name is Mipo E. Dadang. I am a student at Concordia Theological Seminary in Fort Wayne, Indiana, USA. I am pursuing a Doctor of Philosophy in Missiology. I was born and raised in North Central Nigeria where I served as a pastor, in Nigeria for about three decades now. I have served as chaplain, missionary, District Secretary, seminary teacher, national director, West Africa CBSI Director, and the ECWA General Secretary for a maximum two tenures of six years before going to the USA for further studies.

I am now at my last part of my studies and I will be grateful if you will assist me in my research work. This is an additional stage leading to formulating my dissertation. You were randomly selected to ensure that the information reflect the views of the congregations' members in Northern Nigeria. The concern of this study is to find out the approach of congregational members in Northern Nigeria with regards to their response to religious violence in the light of Jesus's teaching and command to love their neighbors. I am optimistic that the result of this study shall help the mission of the church in formulating theological strategies that provide congregational members in Northern Nigeria to have the right approach/response when dealing with the issue of religious violence.

I appreciate your willingness to assist me in my research work. I do promise that your identity or name will not be released in the finished work of this research and no description of your person will be made that could expose your identity as the participants' responses are well coded in this dissertation, except in a situation where your approval is given for me to do so.

APPENDIX THREE

The Demographic Questionnaire

The demographic questions that were asked prior to conducting the interviews to help the researcher in taking note of any characteristics of the participants. Doing this was helpful because the question with regards to personal identity such as name, age, origin (such as place of birth), and religious background (such as years in the Christian faith and what salvation means to a person) are usually helpful for research documentation.

Year of birth: ______________________________

Place of birth: ______________________________

Town: ______________________________

City: ______________________________

For how long have been in the Christian faith? ______________

What Christian role are you involved with? ______________

____

APPENDIX FOUR

Field Research Coding System

Prior to conducting the interviews, the researcher explained clearly toward the last paragraph of his transmittal letter promising that the identity and or names of interviewees will not be released in the finished work of this research dissertation and that no description of their persons would be made that could expose their identity as participants. Responses are well coded in this dissertation without names. In the light of the above explanation, the researcher has devised an easy method of coding of his research work for the participant respondents who were interviewed during the field research work. The first digit is the first alphabet of the respondent's first name and the last three alphabetical letters form the ending letters of the respondent's surname followed by the number which was assigned to all the centers prior and during interviews (for example, EUDA91).

APPENDIX FIVE

Incidents of Provocations against Christians

May 1980: Properties belonging mainly to Christians were destroyed in Zaria

18–29 December 1980: The Maitatsine Muslims sect rose up against Christians in Kano State and killed 4,177 of them and it resulted to extensive destruction of property worth millions of naira.

29–30 October 1982: The Kalamato and Maitatsine Muslim sect in Maiduguri, Borno state, killed 118 Christians and caused extensive damage to property. Muslim demonstrators in Kano state burned down four churches.

27 February to 5 March 1984: Maitatsine Muslim sect in Yola, Adamawa state, killed 586 people in the city and destroyed a lot of property.

26–28 April 1985: Maitatsine Muslim sect in Gombe state killed 105 people and caused extensive destruction of property.

March 1986: Muslims and Christians clashed in Ilorin, Kwara state, during a peaceful Easter procession. There was no recorded death or destruction.

May 1986: In Ibadan, Oyo state, in a demonstration by Muslims they burned the icon of the Risen Christ in the Chapel of Resurrection, University of Ibadan.

6–8 March 1987: In Kafanchan, Kaduna state, clashes between Muslim and Christian students at the College of Education Kafanchan, led to loss of lives and the burning of two mosques by Christian youth. Reprisal in Katsina,

Funtua, Zaria Gusau, and Kaduna, the reprisal of the Kafanchan religious clashes led to Muslims burning twelve churches across the cities mentioned and numerous buildings and property belonging to Christians were destroyed, 125 people died.

February 1988: In Kaduna Polytechnic, religious violence ostensibly around students led to the destruction of the foundation walls of the Christian chapel.

April 1991: In Katsina state, religious violence led by Mallam Yahaya Yakubu, the leader of the fundamentalist Shi'ite sect in Katsina state, in protest to a blasphemous publication in Sun-Times, led to the death of 155 people and destruction of property.

April 1991: In Bauchi state, at Tafawa Balewa, what started as a quarrel between a Fulani man and a Sayawa-Christian meat seller in Tafawa Balewa escalated into a full-blown religious war and spread all over the state capital of Bauchi state.

October 1991: Muslim youth demonstrated against German evangelist Rev. Reinhardt Bonke to prevent Christians from holding a crusade in Kano. It degenerated into very bloody religious violence. Thousands of lives were lost and property valued at millions of naira was destroyed.

February 1992: In Jos, Plateau state, Muslims beat a Christian man to death at Yantaya junction. Christian leaders and pastors worked hard for peace not to breakdown and calmed the situation. There was no retaliation.

15–18 May 1992: In Zangon Kataf, Kaduna state, interreligious war broke out between Muslims and Christians and further spread to the cities of Kaduna destroying several lives and property.

January 1993: Funtua in Katsina state, the Kalakato Muslims religious sect assaulted a village head and burned a police vehicle. Lives were lost and property destroyed.

March 1993: At Angwan Rogo Jos, an area highly populated by Muslims, a twenty-year-old Christian youth was beaten to death. The church leaders and pastors calmed the situation. There was no break of law and order. No mosques or churches were burned.

The 2000 riots were religious riots in Kaduna involving Christians and Muslims over the introduction of sharia law in Kaduna State, Nigeria. The violence happened in two main waves. A first wave from 21 to 25 February, with a further killing in March, followed by a second wave from 22 to 23 May 2000. The death toll was between 2,000 and 5000.

December 2000: In Jos, shortly before Christmas, a Muslim man killed a Christian youth. The Christian leaders and pastors calmed the situation and there was no church or mosque burned.

February 2001: Religious riot broke out in Kaduna. Many Christians were killed. The Baptist College, Kawo-Kaduna, was burned and eight students of the college were killed. This time, many pastors of various churches were killed.

7–12 September 2001: In Jos Plateau state, it was alleged by Muslims that a young girl crossed a public road where Muslims had illegally blocked the road for Jumaat prayer, and that sparked the burning of churches and killing of Christians.

March 2004: Cattle rustlers were said to have raided some cows belonging to a Fulani man. Unfortunately, the Muslims in retaliation killed Christians and destroyed property, churches, and a place of business in Nshar, a small settlement near Shendam in the southern part of Plateau sate. Also in 2004, Muslim youth unleashed terror on every Christian around Angwan Rogo in Jos North when those Christians were returning to their homes from ward congress voting.

December 2007: A Boys Brigade officer, Yakubson, from an ECWA Gospel Church (Tudun Wada, Jos) was returning from a church function along with his colleagues when his throat was slashed opened with knife by a suspected Muslim on a fast motorcycle. He bled to death.

January 2008: A Baptist church in a Christian dominated area, Shendam Plateau state, was burned down by Muslims.

September 2008: A Christian boy was stabbed to death by Muslim youth during Sallah celebration in Jos.

28–30 November 2008: Major religious violence broke out in Jos. In this religious violence, 400 were killed in the city of Jos, and more than 10,000 persons were displaced. Out of the 400 Christians killed, twenty belonged to the ECWA churches, one pastor killed by Muslim youth, thirty-three members were wounded, 202 of the Christians had their homes and property destroyed and looted; and nine ECWA churches were destroyed.

April 2011: Hundreds of Christians were killed and churches burned in regular attacks by Fulani herdsmen in Jos and members of the Boko Haram terrorist sect in Kaduna, Borno, and Niger states. Eight hundred people were killed in the three states mentioned. Thirty-two members and three pastors in the ECWA churches were killed and forty-eight churches burned.

Bibliography

Abashiya, Chris Shu'aibu, and Ayuba Jalaba Ulea. *Christianity and Islam: A Plea for Understanding and Tolerance*. Jos: Holman, 1999.

Accad, Fouad Elias. *Building Bridges: Christianity and Islam*. Colorado Springs: NavPress, 1997.

Adekoya, Olusegun. "The Religious Background" in *Churches in Fellowship: The Story of TEKAN*, edited by Mark Hopkins and Musa Gaiya. Jos: African Christian Textbook, 2005.

Agang, Sunday Bobai. *When Evil Strikes: Faith and the Politics of Human Hostility*. Eugene, Oregon: PICKWICK Publications, 2016.

Agang, Sunday Bobai. *No More Cheeks to Turn?* Carlisle, Cumbria, UK: Hippo books, an imprint of ACTS, Langham Publications, 2017.

Agnes, Michael, ed. *Webster's New World College Dictionary*. 4th ed. New York: Macmillan, 1999.

Alexander, T. Desmond, and Brian S. Rosner, eds. *The New Dictionary of Biblical Theology*. Downers Grove: InterVarsity Press, 2000.

Allen, Roland. *Paul's Missionary Methods: In His Time and Ours*. Updated by Robert L. Plummer and John Mark Terry. Downers Grove: InterVarsity Academic, 2012.

Allison, Dale. "Anticipating the Passion: The Literary Reach of Matthew 26:47–27:56." *The Catholic Biblical Quarterly* 56, no. 4 (1994): 701–14.

Anderson, Norman. *The Teaching of Jesus*. Downers Grove: InterVarsity Press, 1983.

Arnett, Ronald C. *Dwell in Peace: Applying Nonviolence to Every Relationship*. Elgin: Brethren Press, 1980.

Aron, Raymond. *The Century of Total War*. Boston: Beacon Press, 1955.

Augsburger, Myron S. "A Christian Pacifist Response." In *War: Four Christians Views*, edited by Robert G. Clouse, 58–114. Downers Grove: InterVarsity Press, 1981.

Augustine, St. *City of God*. Translated by Gerald G. Walsh. Edited by Vernon J. Bourke. New York: Image Books, 1998.

Ayandele, E. A. *The Missionary Impact on Modern Nigeria*. New York: Humanities Press, 1967.

Bagudu N. Proceedings at the Sir Henry Willinks Commission Appointed to Enquire into the Fears of the Minorities and Means of Allaying Them. Volume 1. Jos: League for Human Rights, 2003.

Barkun, Michael. "Religious Violence and the Myth of Fundamentalism." *Totalitarian Movement and Political Religions* 4, no. 3 (2003): 55–70.

Barnes, A. E. "'Evangelization Where It Was Not Wanted': Colonial Administrators and Missionaries in Northern Nigeria During the First Third of Nineteenth Century." *Journal of Religion in Africa* 25, no. 4 (1995): 412–41.

Barth, Hans-Martin. *The Theology of Martin Luther*. Minneapolis: Fortress, 2013.

Bartleman, Frank. *My Story: "The Latter Rain"*. Columbia, SC: John M. Pike, 1909.

———. *Witness to Pentecost: The Life of Frank Bartleman*. Edited by Donald Dayton. New York: Garland, 1985.

Barrett, David, George T. Kurian, and Todd M. Johnson, eds. *World Christian Encyclopedia*. New York: Oxford University Press, 2001.

Beacham, C. G. "Annual Field Report for Nigeria and French West Africa 1940". *Soul Winning* 17, no. 2 (1941): 1–14.

Bebbington, David W. *Patterns in History: A Christian Perspective on Historical Thought*. Leicester: Apollos, 1990.

Bediako, Kwame. *Theology and Identity: The Impact of Culture Upon Christian Thought in the Second Century and Modern Africa*. Oxford: Regnum, 1992.

Bernard, H. R. *Research Methods in Anthropology: Qualitative and Quantitative Approaches*. 4th ed. Lanham: Altamira Press, 2006.

Best, Shedrach Gaya. *Conflicts and Peace Building in Plateau State*. Ibadan: Spectrum Books, 2007.

Betz, Hans Dieter. *The Sermon on the Mount*. Minneapolis: Fortress, 1995.

Bingham, Rowland. *Seven Sevens and a Jubilee: The Story of Sudan Interior Mission*. Grand Rapids: Zondervan, 1943.

Boer, Jan H. *Christianity and Islam Under Colonialism in Northern Nigeria*. Jos: Institute of Church and Society, 1988.

———. *Nigeria's Decades of Blood*. Studies in Christian-Muslim Relations. Jos: Stream Christian Publishers, 2003.

Bonhoeffer, Dietrich. *The Cost of Discipleship*. New York: Macmillan, 1959.

Booth, Wayne C., Gregory G. Colomb, and Joseph M. Williams. *The Craft of Research*. Chicago: University of Chicago Press, 2003.

Borg, Walter R., Meredith D. Gall, and Joyce P. Gall. *Educational Research: An Introduction*. White Plains: Longman, 1997.

Briscoe, D. Stuart. *The Communicator's Commentary: Romans*. Waco, TX: Word Books, 1982.

Brown, Taylor Barbara. *When God Is Silent*. Cambridge, MA: Cowley, 1998.

Brueggemann, Walter. *Theology of the Old Testament: Testimony, Dispute, Advocacy*. Minneapolis: Fortress, 1997.
Brundage, Anthony. *Going to the Sources: A Guide to Historical Research and Writing*. 4th ed. Wheeling: Harlan Davidson, 2008.
Burgess, Stanley, and Ed M. Van der Mass, eds. *International Dictionary of Pentecostal and Charismatic Movements*. Grand Rapids: Zondervan, 2003.
Cahill, Lisa Sowle. "Danger of Violence and the Call To Peace." In *Strike Terror No More: Theology, Ethics and the New War*, edited by Jon L. Berquist,. Saint Louis: Chalice Press, 2002.
———. *Love Your Enemies: Discipleship, Pacifism and Just War Theory*. Minneapolis: Fortress, 1994.
Cairns, Earle. *Christianity Through Centuries: A History of the Christian Church*. Grand Rapids: Zondervan, 1981.
Canfield, Leon Hardy. *The Early Persecution of Christians*. New York: AMS Press, 1968.
Carson, D. A. "Matthew," In *Matthew, Mark, and Luke*. Vol. 8 of *The Expositor's Bible Commentary*. Grand Rapids: Zondervan, 1984.
Carter, Swaim J. *War: Peace and the Bible*. Maryknoll: Orbis Books, 1982.
Catherine, Marshall. *Designing Qualitative Research*. Thousand Oaks, CA: SAGE Publications, 1995.
Chapman, G. Clarke, Jr. "Terrorism: A Problem for Ethics or Pastoral Theology?" *CrossCurrents* 54, no. 1 (2004): 120–37.
Chernus, Ira. *American Nonviolence: The History of an Idea*. Maryknoll: Orbis Books, 2004.
Chilton, Bruce. *Abraham's Curse: The Root of Violence in Judaism, Christianity and Islam*. New York: Doubleday, 2008.
Clapsis, Emmanuel, ed. *Violence and Christian Spirituality: An Ecumenical Conversation*. Geneva: WCC Publications, 2007.
Clouse, Robert G., ed. *War: Four Christian Views*. Downers Grove: InterVarsity Press, 1981.
Cole, Durrell. *When God Says War Is Right: The Christian's Perspective on When and How to Fight*. Colorado Springs: Waterbrook Press, 2002.
Collier, Rosalyn Falcon, Ann E. Helmke, Laura R. Holck. Walking Jesus' Path of Peace *Living Faithfully in a Violent World*. Minneapolis: Augsburg Fortress, 2001.
Conquest, Robert. *Reflections on a Ravaged Century*. New York: Norton, 2001.
Cooper, Barbara M. *Evangelical Christians in the Muslim Sahel*. Bloomington: Indiana University Press, 2006.
Copan, Paul. *Is God a Moral Monster? Making Sense of the Old Testament God*. Grand Rapids: Baker Books, 2011.

Cox, Harvey G. *Fire from Heaven: The Rise of Pentecostal Spirituality and Reshaping of Religion in the Twenty-First Century*. Reading: Addison-Wesley, 1995.

Crampton, Edward Patrick Thurman. *Christianity in Northern Nigeria*. Zaria: Gaskiya Corporation Publication, 1975.

———. *Christianity in Northern Nigeria*. 2nd ed. London: Chapman, 1979.

Creech, Joe. *Righteous Indignation: Religion and the Populist Revolution*. Urbana: University of Illinois Press, 2006.

Creswell, John W. *Research Design: Qualitative, Quantitative and Mixed Methods Approaches.* 3rd ed. London: SAGE, 2009.

Culliton, Joseph T. *Nonviolence, Central to Christian Spirituality: Perspectives from Scripture to the Present*. New York: Edwin Mellen Press, 1982.

Culver, Robert Duncan. *The Peace Mongers: A Biblical Answer to Pacifism and Nuclear Disarmament*. Wheaton: Tyndale House Publishers, 1985.

Dadang, Mipo Ezekiel. *Anger and Forgiveness: How Can You Win the Battle?* Bukuru: Africa Christian Textbooks, 2018.

———. 125 Years of Serving in Mission (SIM) in Nigeria: A Missiological-theological Appraisal of Missionary Work. *Theological Journal for Church and Society* 1, no. 1 (2020): 53–77.

Daschke, Dereck, and D. Andrew Kille. *A Cry Instead of Justice: The Bible and Cultures in Psychological Perspective*. New York: T &T Clark, 2010.

Das, Sisir Kumar. *The Shadow of the Cross: Christianity and Hinduism in a Colonial Situation*. New Delhi: Munshiram Manoharlal, 1971.

Dear, John. *Living Peace: A Spirituality of Contemplation and Action*. New York: Doubleday, 2001.

De Gruchy, John W. *Reconciliation: Restoring Justice*. Minneapolis: Fortress Press, 2002.

Descombe, Martyn. *The Good Research Guide: For Small-Scale Social Research Projects*. Buckingham, PA: Open University Press, 2000.

Dietrich, Walter. "The Mark of Cain: Violence and Overcoming Violence in the Hebrew Bible." *Theology Digest* 52 (2005): 3–11.

Eitel, Keith E., ed. *Missions in Contexts of Violence*. Pasadena: William Carey Library, 2008.

Elford, R. John. "Christianity and War." In *The Cambridge Companion to Christian Ethics*, edited by Robin Gill, 170–82. Cambridge: Cambridge University Press, 2001.

Elliot, Julia, Hawker, Sara & Soames, Catherine. *Dictionary of Current English*. Oxford: Oxford University Press, 2006.

Elliston, Edgar J. *Introduction to Missiological Research Design*. Pasadena: William Carey Library, 2011.

Engelbrecht, Edward A. *The Lutheran Study Bible: English Standard Version*. Saint Louis: Concordia, 2009.

Erickson, Victoria Lee, and Michelle Lim Jones, eds. *Surviving Terror: Hope and Justice in a World of Violence*. Grand Rapids, MI: Brazos, 2002.

Faught, C. Brad. "Missionaries, Indirect Rule and the Changing Mandate of Mission in Colonial Northern Nigeria: The Case of Canada's Rowland Victor Bingham and the Sudan Interior Mission." *Journal of Canadian Church Historical Society* 43, no. 2 (2001): 147–69.

Feinberg, C. L. "Peace." In *Evangelical Dictionary of Theology*, edited by Walter Elwell, 896. Grand Rapids: Eerdmans, 1983.

Ferguson, John. *The Politics of Love: The New Testament and Nonviolent Revolution*. Cambridge: James Clarke, 1973.

Fiedler, Klaus. *The Story of Faith Missions: From Hudson Taylor to Present Day Africa*. Oxford: Regnum, 1994.

Flint, John. *Sir George Goldie and the Making of Nigeria*. Oxford: Oxford University Press, 1960.

France, R. T. *The Gospel of Matthew*. Grand Rapids: Eerdmans, 2007

Fretheim, Terrence E. "'I Was Only a Little Angry': Divine Violence in the Prophets." *Interpretation* 58, no. 4 (2004): 365–75.

Fuller, W. Harold. *Mission-Church Dynamics: How To Change Bicultural Tension into Dynamic Missionary Outreach*. Pasadena: William Carey Library, 1980.

Gates, Henry Louis, and Kwame Anthony Appiah. *Africana: The Encyclopedia of the African and African American Experience*. New York: Basic Civitas Books, 1999.

Gehman, Richard J. *African Traditional Religion in the Light of the Bible*. Jos: African Christian Textbooks, 2001.

Gibbs, Jeffrey A. *Matthew 1:1–11:1*. Concordia Commentary. Saint Louis: Concordia, 2006.

Gilbert, Lela, and Paul A. Marshall. *Their Blood Cries Out: The Worldwide Tragedy of Modern Christians Who Are Dying for Their Faith*. Dallas: Word Publishing, 1997.

Gill, D W. "Violence." In *The New Dictionary of Christian Ethics and Pastoral Theology*, edited by Atkinson, David, and David Field, 875–879. Leicester: Inter-Varsity Press, 1995.

Gill, Robin, ed. *The Cambridge Companion to Christian Ethics*. Cambridge: Cambridge University Press, 2001.

Gofwen, Rotgak I. *Religious Conflicts in Northern Nigeria and Nation Building: The Theories of Two Decades 1980–2000*. Kaduna, Nigeria: Human Rights Monitor, 2004.

Grant, Michael. *The World of Rome*. London: Weidenfeld and Nicolson, 1994.

Griffith, Lee. *The War on Terrorism and the Terror of God*. Grand Rapids: Eerdmans, 2004.

Gutip, Nanwul. *Church of Christ in Nigeria COCIN: Birth and Growth*. Jos: Crossroads Communicators, 1998.

Haak, Robert D. "Mapping Violence in the Prophets: Zechariah 2." In *The Aesthetics of Violence in the Prophets*, edited by Julia M. O'Brien and Chris Franke, 18–36. New York: T & T Clark, 2010.

Harrington Watt, David. "The Meaning and End of Fundamentalism." *Religious Studies Review* 30, no. 4 (2004): 271–74.

Harrison, Everett F. *Baker's Dictionary of Theology*. Grand Rapids: Baker Books, 1960.

Hastings, Adrian. *A World History of Christianity*. Grand Rapids: Eerdmans, 1999.

Hauerwas, Stanley. "Christian Nonviolence." In *Strike Terror No More: Theology, Ethics and the New War*, edited by Jon L. Berquist, 245–247. Saint Louis: Chalice, 2002.

Hecht, Bill. *Two Wars: We Must Not Lose*. Fort Wayne: Concordia Theological Seminary Press, 2012.

Hengel, Martin. *Victory Over Violence: Jesus and Revolutionists*. Philadelphia: Fortress, 1973.

Herbert, Schlossberg. *Called to Suffer, Called to Triumph: Eighteen True Stories by Persecuted Christians*. Portland: Multnomah, 1990.

Hiebert, Paul G. *Anthropological Insights for Missionaries*. Grand Rapids, MI: Baker Books, 1985.

Hollenweger, Walter J. *Pentecostalism: Origins and Developments Worldwide*. Peabody: Hendrickson, 1997.

Hornus, Jean Michel. *It Is Not Lawful for Me to Fight*. Scottsdale: Herald Press, 1980.

Hunter, John H. *A Flame of Fire: The Life and Work of Rowland Victor Bingham*. Toronto: Sudan Interior Mission, 1961.

Huntington, S. P. *The Clash of Civilizations and the Remaking of the World Order*. London: Touchstone, 1996.

Hurlbut, Jesse Lyman. *The Story of the Christian Church*. Grand Rapids: Zondervan, 1979.

Idowu, E. Bolaji. *Olodumare: God in Yoruba Belief*. London: Longman, 1962.

Inrig, Gary. *Forgiveness*. Grand Rapids: Discovery House Publishers, 2005.

Irvin, Dale. "The Terror of History and the Memory of Redemption: Engaging the Ambiguities of the Christian Past." In *Surviving Terror: Hope and Justice in a World of Violence*, edited by Victoria Lee Erickson and Michelle Lim Jones, 10–63. Grand Rapids: Brazos, 2002.

Isichei, Elizabeth. *A History of Christianity in Africa: From Antiquity to the Present*. Grand Rapids: Eerdmans, 1995.

Jacobsen, Douglas. *The World's Christians: Who They Are, Where They Are, and How They Got There*. Chichester: Willey-Blackwell, 2007.

Janvier, George. *How to Write a Theological Research Thesis*. Jos: African Christian Textbooks, 2000.

Johnson, Roger A. *Peacemaking and Religious Violence: From Thomas Aquinas to Thomas Jefferson*. London: Lutterworth, 2011.

Johnstone, Patrick, and Jason Mandryk. *Operation World*. Carlisle: Paternoster, 2001.

Just, Arthur A. *Luke 9:51–24:53*. Concordia Commentary. Saint Louis: Concordia, 1997.

Kalu, O. Ogbu. *African Pentecostalism: An Introduction*. Oxford: Oxford University Press, 2008.

———. "Jesus Christ, Where Are You? Themes in West African Church Historiography at the Edge of the 21st Century." *Missionalia* 30, no. 2 (2002): 235–64.

Karl, Rahner. *Encounter with Silence*. 5th ed. Westminster: Newman Press, 1965.

Kassmann, Margot. *Overcoming Violence: The Challenge to the Churches in All Places*. Geneva: WCC Publications, 1998.

Kastfelt, Niels. *Religion and Politics in Nigeria: A Study in Middle Belt Christianity*. London: British Academic Press, 1994.

Keener, Craig S. *A Commentary on the Gospel of Matthew*. Grand Rapids: Eerdmans, 1999.

———. *The IVP Bible Background Commentary: New Testament*. Downers Grove: InterVarsity Press, 1993.

———. *Gift Givers Holy Spirit for Today*. Grand Rapids: Baker Academic, 2001.

Kleinig, John W. *Leviticus*. Concordia Commentary. Saint Louis: Concordia, 2004.

Kober, Ted. *Confessions and Forgiveness: Professing Faith as Ambassadors of Reconciliation*. Saint Louis: Concordia, 2002.

Kolb, Robert, and Timothy J. Wengert, eds. *The Book of Concord: The Confessions of the Evangelical Lutheran Church*. Minneapolis: Augsburg Fortress, 2001.

———, eds. *The Book of Concord: The Confessions of the Evangelical Lutheran Church*. Translated by Charles Arand. Minneapolis: Augsburg Fortress, 2004.

Koschorke, Klaus, Frieder Ludwig, and Mariano Delgado, eds. *A History of Christianity in Asia, Africa and Latin America 1450–1990*. Grand Rapids: Eerdmans, 2007.

Kreider, Alan, Eleanor Kreider, and Paulus Widjaja. *A Culture of Peace: God's Vision for the Church*. Intercourse: Good Books, 2005.

Kukah, Matthew Hassan. "Christians and Nigeria's Aborted Transition." In *The Christian Churches and the Democratization of Africa*, edited by Paul Gifford, 225–38. Leiden: Brill, 1995.

Kunhiyop, Samuel Waje. *African Christian Ethics*. Grand Rapids: World Alive, 2008.

Laetsch, Theodore. *The Minor Prophets*. Saint Louis: Concordia, 1965.

Lageer, E. *New Life for All: True Accounts of In-Depth Evangelism in West Africa*. Chicago: Moody Press, 1969.
Levin, Michael D. "The New Nigeria: Displacement and the Nation." In *Displacement and the Politics of Violence in Nigeria*, edited by Paul Ellsworth Lovejoy and Pat Ama Tokunbo Williams, 134–44. Leiden: Brill, 1997.
Long, Edward Leroy. *Peace Thinking in a Warring World*. Philadelphia: Westminster, 1983.
Lorenz, Eckhart. *Justice Through Violence?: Ethical Criteria for Legitimate Use of Force*. Geneva: Lutheran World Federation, 1984.
Loves, Yahweh. *The Beginning of the End of Islam on the Plateau*. Jos: Savior's Associates, 2010.
Luther, Martin. *Luther's Works: The Career of the Reformer*. Vol. 31. Edited by Harold J. Grimm. Philadelphia: Fortress, 1957.
———. *Luther's Works: The Christian in Society II*. Vol. 45. Edited by Walther I. Brandt and Helmut T. Lehmann. Philadelphia: Muhlenberg Press, 1962.
———. *Luther's Works: The Christian in Society III*. Vol. 46. Edited by Robert Schultz. Philadelphia: Fortress, 1967.
———. *Luther's Works: Church and Ministry II*. Vol. 40. Edited by Conrad Bergendoff and Helmut T. Lehmann. Philadelphia: Fortress Press, 1958.
———. *Luther's Works: Lectures on Deuteronomy*. Vol. 9. Edited by Jaroslav Pelikan and Daniel Poellot. Sain Louis: Concordia Publishing House, 1960.
———. *Luther's Works: Word and Sacrament*. Vol. 35. Edited by Theodore Bachmann. Philadelphia: Fortress, 1960.
Macgregor, G. H. C. *The New Testament Basis for Pacifism and the Relevance of an Impossible Ideal*. New York: Fellowship Publications, 1954.
Marshall, Michael. *The Restless Heart: The Life and Influence of St. Augustine*. Grand Rapids: Eerdmans, 1987.
Marshall, Paul. "Persecution of Christians in the Contemporary World." *International Bulletin of Missionary Research* 22, no. 1 (January 1998): 2–8.
Maxwell, Joseph. *Qualitative Research Design: Interactive Approach*. Thousand Oaks: SAGE, 1996.
McEntire, Mark. *The Blood of Abel: The Violent Plot in the Hebrew Bible*. Macon: Mercer University Press, 1979.
Merton, Thomas. *Peace in the Post-Christian Era*. Maryknoll: Orbis Books, 2004.
Middleton Richard. "Violence." In *The New Interpreter's Dictionary of the Bible. Vol. 5*, edited by Katharine Doob Sakenfield, 783–784. Nashville: Abingdon Press, 2009.
Midgely, Graham. *The Miscellaneous Works of John Bunyan*. Vol. 5, *The Barren Fig Tree, the Strait Gate, and the Heavenly Foot-Man*. Oxford: Clarendon, 1986.
Mieth, Dietmar, and Maria Pilar Aquino. *The Return to Just War*. London: SCM Press, 2001.

Milgrom, Jacob. *Leviticus 17–22*. Anchor Bible Commentary. New York: Doubleday, 2000.

Miller, William Robert. *Nonviolent: A Christian Interpretation*. New York: Schoken Books, 1996.

Minchakpu, Obed. "Eye for an Eye: Christians Avenge February Murder, Spark Muslim Retaliation." *Christianity Today* 48, no. 7 (2004): 17

Mowatt, Harriet and John Swinton. *Practical Theology and Qualitative Research*. London: SCM, 2006.

Neil, Stephen. *A History of Christian Missions*. Harmondsworth: Penguin Books, 1986.

Noll, Mark A. *A History of Christianity in the United States and Canada*. Grand Rapids: Eerdmans, 1992.

———. *The Scandal of the Evangelical Mind*. Leicester: Inter-Varsity Press, 1994.

Nyber, Richard. "Pastors Killed, Churches Burned: New Wave of Violence Begins." *Christianity Today* 48, no. 6 June (2004): 17.

Oguntola, Sunday. "No More Cheeks to Turn: Nigerian Christians Abandon Check-Turning." *Christianity Today* 55, no. 12 (2011): 14.

Okorocha, Cyril C. "Religious Conversion in Africa: Its Missiological Implications." *Mission Studies* 9, no. 1 (1992): 168–81.

Okwori, E. Moses. *Godliness for Gain: A Theological Evaluation of the Nigerian Version of the Prosperity Gospel*. Jos: Tony Kes Press, 1995.

Olatayo, David I. *ECWA: The Root, Birth, and Growth, Book 1*. Ilorin: Ocare Publications, 1993.

———. *ECWA: The Root, Birth, and Growth, Book 2*. Ilorin: Ocare Publications, 1993.

Osaghae, E. E., and R. T. Suberu. *A History of Identities, Violence and Stability in Nigeria*. Ibadan: Center for Research and Inequality, 2003.

Otite, B. A., and Williwam Ogionwo. *An Introduction to Sociological Studies*. Ibadan: Heinemann Educational, 1979.

Oyewole, A. *Historical Dictionary of Nigeria*. African Historical Dictionaries. Metuchen: Scarecrow Press, 1987.

Pape, Robert A. *Dying to Win: The Strategic Logic of Suicide Terrorism*. New York: Random House, 2005.

Parrinder, Edward Geoffrey. *West African Religion*. London: Epworth Press, 1961.

Patton, Michael Quinn. *Qualitative Research and Evaluation Methods*. 3rd ed. Thousand Oaks: SAGE, 2001.

Pocock, Michael. *The Changing Face of World Missions*. Grand Rapids: Baker Academic, 2005.

Rahner, Karl. *Encounter with Silence*. 5th ed. Westminster: The Newman Press, 1965.

Roehrs, Walter R. *Concordia Self-Study Commentary*. Saint Louis: Concordia Publishing House, 1971.

Sanneh, Lamin. *Translating the Message: The Missionary Impact on Culture*. Maryknoll: Orbis Books, 1989

Scaer, David P. *Sermon on the Mount: The Church's First Statement of the Gospel*. Saint Louis: Concordia, 2000.

Schulz, Klaus Detlev. *Mission from the Cross: The Lutheran Theology of Missions*. Saint Louis: Concordia, 2009.

Sider, Ronald J. "How Should Christians Respond?" In *Strike Terror No More: Theology, Ethics and the New War*, edited by Jon L. Berquist, 326–28. Saint Louis: Chalice, 2002

Smart, Ninian. *Dimensions of the Sacred: An Anatomy of World's Beliefs*. Berkeley: University of California Press, 1996.

Stanley, Brian. *The Bible and Flag: Protestant Missions and British Imperialism in the Nineteenth and Twentieth Centuries*. Leicester: Inter-Varsity Press, 1990.

Steinbronn, Anthony J. *Worldviews: A Christian Response to Religious Pluralism*. Saint Louis: Concordia, 2007.

Stott, John. *Men with a Message: An Introduction to the New Testament and Its Writers*. Grand Rapids: Eerdmans, 1994.

———. The Message of the Sermon on the Mount: Christian Counter-Culture. Downers Grove: Illinois University Press, 1978.

Stumme, John R., and Karen L. Bloomquist. "Introduction: A Tradition of Ethics in Today's Context." In *The Promise of Lutheran Ethics*, edited by Karen L. Bloomquist and John R. Stumme, 1–11. Minneapolis: Augsburg Fortress, 1998.

Sundita, Abbas. *Look Behind the Façade: Some Serious Stuff You're Not Supposed to Know About Islam*. Maitland: Xulon Press, 2006.

Susin, Luiz Carlos, and Maria Pilar Aquino, eds. *Reconciliation in a World of Conflicts*. London: SCM Press, 2003.

Synon, Vinson. *The Holiness-Pentecostal Tradition: Charismatic Movements in the Twentieth Century*. Grand Rapids: Eerdmans, 1997.

Thompson, Joseph Milburn. *Justice and Peace: A Christian Primer*. Maryknoll: Orbis Books, 2003.

Tsetsis, Georges. "Non-Violence in the Orthodox Tradition." In *Violence and Christian Spirituality: An Ecumenical Conversation*, edited by Emmanuel Clapsis, 56–62. Geneva, Switzerland: WCC Publications, 2007.

Tucker, Ruth A. "Rowland Bingham and the Sudan Interior Mission." In *From Jerusalem to Irian Jaya: Biographical History of Christian Missions*, 295–99. Grand Rapids: Zondervan, 1983.

Ubah, C. N. "Colonial Administration and the Spread of Islam in Northern Nigeria." *The Muslim World* 81, no. 2 (1991): 133–48.

Vanderhaar, Gerard A. *Christians and Nonviolence in the Nuclear Age: Scripture, the Arms Race, and You*. Mystic: Twenty-Third Publications, 1982.

Van Rheenen, Gailyn, ed. *Contextualization and Syncretism: Navigating Cultural Currents*. Pasadena: William Carey Library, 2006.

Vicedom, Georg F. *The Mission of God: An Introduction to a Theology of Mission*. Translated by Gilbert A. Thiele and Dennis Hilgendorf. Saint Louis: Concordia, 1965.

Volf, Miroslav. *Exclusion and Embrace: A Theological Exploration of Identity, Otherness, and Reconciliation*. Nashville: Abingdon, 1996.

Wacker, Grant. *Heaven Below: Early Pentecostals and American Culture*. Cambridge, MA: Harvard University Press, 2001.

Wacker, Grant, and Augustus Cerillo, Jr. "Bibliography and Historiography of Pentecostalism in the United States." In *The New International Dictionary of Pentecostalism and Charismatic Movements*, edited by Stanley Burgess, 69. Grand Rapids: Zondervan, 2002.

Walls, Andrew F. *The Cross-Cultural Process in Christian History: Studies in the Transmission and Appropriation of Faith*. Maryknoll: Orbis Books, 2002.

———. *The Missionary Movement in Christian History: Studies in the Transmission of Faith*. Maryknoll: Orbis, 2009.

Walther, C. F. W. *The Proper Distinction between Law and Gospel*. Saint Louis, MO: Concordia, 1986.

Waltke, Bruce K. *Old Testament Theology: An Exegetical Canonical and Thematic Approach*. Grand Rapids: Zondervan, 2007.

Weber, Timothy P. *Living in the Shadow of the Second Coming*. New York: Oxford University Press, 1979.

Witherington, Ben. *The Acts of the Apostles: A Socio-Rhetorical Commentary*. Grand Rapids: Eerdmans, 1998.

Wikipedia. S.v. "Sahelian Kingdoms." Last modified 24 April 2021, http://en.wikipedia.org/wiki/Sahelian_kingdoms.

Wilson Trigg, Joseph. *Origen: The Bible and Philosophy in the Third-Century*. London: SCM Press, 1985

Windass, Stan. *Christianity Versus Violence: A Social Study of War and Christianity*. London: Sheed and Ward, 1964.

Wink, Walter. Engaging the Powers: Discernment and Resistance in a World of Domination. Minneapolis: Fortress, 1992.

———. *Jesus and Nonviolence: A Third Way*. Minneapolis: Fortress, 2003.

Langham Literature, with its publishing work, is a ministry of Langham Partnership.

Langham Partnership is a global fellowship working in pursuit of the vision God entrusted to its founder John Stott –

> ***to facilitate the growth of the church in maturity and Christ-likeness through raising the standards of biblical preaching and teaching.***

Our vision is to see churches in the Majority World equipped for mission and growing to maturity in Christ through the ministry of pastors and leaders who believe, teach and live by the word of God.

Our mission is to strengthen the ministry of the word of God through:

- nurturing national movements for biblical preaching
- fostering the creation and distribution of evangelical literature
- enhancing evangelical theological education

especially in countries where churches are under-resourced.

Our ministry

Langham Preaching partners with national leaders to nurture indigenous biblical preaching movements for pastors and lay preachers all around the world. With the support of a team of trainers from many countries, a multi-level programme of seminars provides practical training, and is followed by a programme for training local facilitators. Local preachers' groups and national and regional networks ensure continuity and ongoing development, seeking to build vigorous movements committed to Bible exposition.

Langham Literature provides Majority World preachers, scholars and seminary libraries with evangelical books and electronic resources through publishing and distribution, grants and discounts. The programme also fosters the creation of indigenous evangelical books in many languages, through writer's grants, strengthening local evangelical publishing houses, and investment in major regional literature projects, such as one volume Bible commentaries like the *Africa Bible Commentary* and the *South Asia Bible Commentary*.

Langham Scholars provides financial support for evangelical doctoral students from the Majority World so that, when they return home, they may train pastors and other Christian leaders with sound, biblical and theological teaching. This programme equips those who equip others. Langham Scholars also works in partnership with Majority World seminaries in strengthening evangelical theological education. A growing number of Langham Scholars study in high quality doctoral programmes in the Majority World itself. As well as teaching the next generation of pastors, graduated Langham Scholars exercise significant influence through their writing and leadership.

To learn more about Langham Partnership and the work we do visit **langham.org**